FIGHT FOR
FALKLANDS
FREEDOM

FIGHT FOR FALKLANDS FREEDOM

Reporting Live from Argentina and the Islands

HAROLD BRILEY

No one in Buenos Aires had a more helpful attitude to the Islanders than Harold Briley. He did a terrific job keeping up morale. The Falkland Islands expressed their appreciation with a huge banner saying 'God Bless you, Harold!'

Sir Rex Hunt, Falklands Governor, 1982

Harold Briley is one of the best and wisest correspondents – very sound on the Falklands.

Lord Shackleton, pioneer of Falklands post-war prosperity

Harold Briley in every corner of the world has been one of the best Correspondents I have ever met and the most well-informed. In good times and in bad, we never had a bad word.

Lord Carrington, who resigned as Foreign Secretary

Your voice from Buenos Aires loomed large to us at Ten Downing Street.

Hugh Colver (Ministry of Defence Public Relations Chief and aide to Prime Minister)

Thanks to Harold Briley from all of us in the Armed Services for his support and perceptive reporting.

General Sir Peter de la Billière (UK Commandant of SAS during Falklands War)

To our Man in Buenos Aires. Thank you for keeping
our end up.

Admiral of the Fleet Lord Lewin (Chief of Defence Staff, 1982)

Harold Briley's Falklands war coverage was one of the
most extended pieces of sustained stamina of any
correspondent on any story.

Sir John Tusa (Director, BBC World Service)

There was continuous praise here for the BBC's
magnificent coverage ... the only reliable news media.
Special thanks to Harold Briley. He was outstanding.

1982 Telegram from Islanders leaders, signed Harold Rowlands
(Chief Government Official)

Your Newsletters were a source of great comfort to us
in our darkest days during Argentine occupation.

Falkland Islands Association Committee, Stanley

Your heartening reports from enemy territory did a lot
to boost the morale of the Falkland Islanders. We will
never forget you.

Falkland Islands Club

This book is dedicated to the Falkland Islanders
and to the British Armed Forces whose
courage and sacrifice liberated them.

The author will make a donation for every copy sold to research
by forces' charities into post-traumatic stress disorder (PTSD)
from which many Falklands and other veterans suffer.

First published 2022

The History Press
97 St George's Place, Cheltenham,
Gloucestershire, GL50 3QB
www.thehistorypress.co.uk

British Library Cataloguing in Publication Data.
A catalogue record for this book is available from the British Library.

ISBN 978 0 7509 9953 3

Typesetting and origination by The History Press
Printed and bound by TJ Books Limited, Padstow, Cornwall

Trees for L♔fe

MIX
Paper from
responsible sources
FSC
www.fsc.org   FSC® C013056

CONTENTS

SECTION THREE: THE MEDIA AND THE WAR OF WORDS

SECTION FOUR: 1982–2022 RECOVERY AND AFTERMATH

SECTION FIVE: EARLY HISTORY,
ORIGINS OF DISPUTE

FOREWORD

By Sir John Tusa, former Director of BBC World Service.

This book is a comprehensive account of the 1982 Falklands Conflict, not just the fighting but all the events influencing the dispute – political, diplomatic and historical, from its origins centuries ago to the present day. Front-line reports give eyewitness descriptions of what happened and the far-reaching consequences for Britain, Argentina and the Falkland Islands.

The author and his colleagues won widespread acclaim, which countered criticism of some BBC broadcasts from the Prime Minister and military commanders for disclosing troop and ship deployments. The BBC repudiated these criticisms, defending its hard-won commitment to give accurate accounts of events, however unpalatable. The book reveals both British and Argentine sources crediting BBC reports of British advances persuading Argentine commanders to surrender, thus shortening the war and saving lives.

BBC World Service radio overcame communication obstacles to reach where other media could not. These were 'truly the first drafts of history'. The Islanders sent many messages of thanks to the BBC and to Harold Briley for reports which kept them informed and boosted morale.

He was uniquely qualified to communicate with them in a personal way, having visited the Islands the year before the invasion, forging lasting friendships in scattered farm communities.

I paid him this tribute: 'Harold Briley's Falklands war coverage was one of the most extended pieces of sustained stamina of any correspondent on any story.'

For four years, he reported events in a vast area of 8 million square miles from Mexico to the Antarctic through twenty-five countries, most of them hostile military regimes.

His reports brought death threats from Argentine hit squads who kidnapped and killed 120 journalists and arrested others. He was forced to quit Argentina for a time but defied the death threats to return to Buenos Aires to broadcast globally the first news of the invasion, followed by hundreds more during and after the conflict.

He was in the right place at the right time. Foresight, as well as courage and stamina, is the hallmark of a good foreign correspondent.

If luck matters too, a good correspondent makes his own. Harold Briley certainly did – and deserved it.

John Tusa

(Explanatory note: War was never officially declared by Argentina or the United Kingdom. So, it was called a 'conflict'. But, by any other name, it was war, deploying all the weapons of war: shot and shell, artillery and aircraft, ship and submarine, tanks and troops, bomb and bayonet, mortar, missile and mine.)

SETTING THE SCENE
– CAUSES AND
CONSEQUENCES –
PAST AND PRESENT

The Full Story: Invasion, History, People, Politics.

It began with a surprise dawn invasion on 2 April 1982, shattering the peace of a neglected British colony, the Falkland Islands – an isolated cluster of islands 8,000 miles away in the South Atlantic and only 300 miles from Argentina. A population of 1,800 had been engaged in sheep farming for more than a century in a penguin paradise that was teeming with wildlife. Having visited them fifteen months earlier, I feared for their safety when they were inundated by an Argentine armada of ships, warplanes and 10,000 troops.

Years of negotiations with the United Kingdom for transfer of sovereignty were abruptly halted by a desperate dictatorship acting to stall its downfall by rebellion by a population protesting against corruption, economic hardship and brutal repression. But its attempt to unite the nation by satisfying a long-cherished ambition to possess the Islands failed. The UK sent a powerful navy-led task force to recapture the Islands.

Appeasement of Argentina by Britain deliberately left them defenceless. The UK continued selling deadly weapons to the enemy for which they never paid! The UK contemplated betraying the Islanders to a cruel regime, telling them they would be 'better off' as part of Argentina! Thirty years earlier, Winston Churchill had acted decisively to deter Argentine ambition.

Margaret Thatcher told me on a visit to the Falkland Islands that the invasion came as a complete surprise. Yet the government's military intelligence services warned of the Argentine threat many times over several years. Argentina even publicly announced – and told me in advance – that its deadline was January 1983 to gain possession.

The Prime Minister said the worst decision in her life was to send men to war knowing some of them would be killed. She took the risky decision solely on the judgement of one man: the Head of the Navy, Admiral Sir Henry Leach, whose foresight had his ships ready to sail. Margaret Thatcher's political career was saved by the Admiral's military acumen.

A war of words, not just of weapons, weaved a web of lies, distortion, diplomatic deception, and even an allegation accusing the British Ambassador in Buenos Aires of helping the enemy because he favoured Argentina.

The invasion forced a reversal of UK policy, in future to pledge total support for the Islands' defence, development and determination to remain British.

The intriguing question persists: *what if …?*

If Argentina had won, the dictatorship would have survived and triggered another war by invading Chile. The dictators would have escaped lifetime jail sentences for human rights atrocities. The Falkland Islanders would have emigrated, mostly to New Zealand. And the Thatcher government would have been brought down.

Nearly 1,000 people killed in the conflict would have died in vain. They, above all, were the losers.

Who were the winners? The British armed forces, for their determination and courage. And the Falkland Islanders, who have since built a dynamic, democratic country, energised by a highly educated post-conflict generation occupying key roles in government and commerce.

The Falklands saga reads like far-fetched fiction. But it is realistic fact, which this book clarifies, telling the story word by word of what happened as it happened, from the author's own on-the-spot experience, supplemented by secret documents since declassified.

The seventy-four-day conflict did not end one of the longest sovereignty disputes in history. Forty years on, Argentina continues to intensify its claim. And the United Kingdom emphatically rejects it.

In the six months leading up to the 40th anniversary, Argentina was again in political crisis, the UK updated its progress on building a stronger navy, and the Falklands government revealed far-reaching plans for economic development – a very different scenario from 1982.

Harold Briley, 2021

SECTION ONE:
PATH TO WAR

1

DATELINE BUENOS AIRES

Foreign Office tells Governor, 'Make your dispositions accordingly!'

Invasion came suddenly at first light, spearheaded by special forces. As they splashed ashore from landing craft, I was in Buenos Aires broadcasting first news of the invasion on the BBC World Service to a global audience, most of whom had never heard of the Falkland Islands. Newsflashes from Reuters and other international agencies were dropping on editors' desks worldwide.

Here's what I broadcast at this dramatic moment:

BBC despatch, Argentine Invasion: Falklands 02/04/1982, 0600 GMT

CUE: Argentina's threatened invasion of the British Colony, the Falkland Islands, is reported to be under way. A fleet headed by Argentina's flagship *Veintecinco de Mayo* (25th of May) was reported to be heading the invasion assault in which thousands of troops and aircraft were taking part. Official confirmation was expected from the President, General Leopoldo Galtieri, in a nationwide television and radio broadcast. From Buenos Aires, a report by BBC Latin America Correspondent Harold Briley.

'The assault on the islands was timed to begin at first light with a commando raid to take possession of the airport just outside the capital, Port Stanley. The plan was to pour thousands of troops ashore and swiftly secure the islands, inhabited by eighteen hundred British people. Some reports say troops have landed and are advancing from the airport but there is no official confirmation. A token force of about eighty British marines commanded by a major was braced to fight back but with little chance against such heavy odds. The invasion fleet was said to number several ships, the aircraft carrier, several destroyers and corvettes, and submarines.

'The only British navy ship in the area, patrolling off the Falklands dependency of South Georgia, a thousand miles south-east of the main islands, was the ice patrol vessel *Endurance*, armed with only two light guns and two helicopters. But a powerful British fleet was said to have put to sea, headed by Britain's newest aircraft carrier, *Invincible*, but with a long way to go.

'The fateful decision to go ahead with the threatened invasion first came soon after midnight with an Argentine news agency report. It said the invasion force was on the way and that the Army Chief of Operations, General Mario Menéndez, has been named as Military Governor of the islands, with three other senior officers to help him.

'The Argentine aircraft carrier was reported to have fifteen hundred assault troops on board, and many more, including airborne troops, had been mobilised in the southern ports of Rio Gallegos and Comodoro Rivadavia, facing the islands about three hundred miles away in the South Atlantic. The invasion was timed to take place before British naval reinforcements would arrive in a dash of several thousands of miles across the Atlantic from Europe. As dawn came here in Buenos Aires, the air was filled with the sound of military aircraft flying overhead.'

Harold Briley, BBC, Buenos Aires.

Journalists are said to write the first rough drafts of history. But I was only the messenger. The message had been written thirty years earlier in Argentina's invasion plan, repeatedly updated since.

The Governor of the Falkland Islands, Rex Hunt, with communications to the outside world cut off, told me he listened to my broadcast crouched under a table in Government House, radio beside him and revolver in hand to repel Argentine intruders. 'As I listened to you,' he said, 'Argentine troops arrived, shooting out all the windows in my conservatory.' The Falklands were in the front line and on the front pages when much of the world never knew they existed.

The first intimation of invasion came in a Foreign Office cable to the Governor: 'An Argentine task force will gather on Cape Pembroke (the approach to Port Stanley) early tomorrow morning, 2 April. You will wish to make your dispositions accordingly.'

The Governor's communications officer, Brian Wells, tore the cable from the printer with the cheery remark, 'They might have added "Goodbye – and the best of British [luck] …!"'

UK foreign policies had placed the Falkland Islands in a perilous predicament. Indecision and appeasement had prevented military reinforcement as 'unjustifiable expense'. The irony is that the procrastination of the past would immeasurably multiply the cost for the future – £3.5 billion for the ten-week war and tens of millions every year since for recovery and defence.

As commander-in-chief as well as governor, Rex Hunt's 'dispositions', as the Foreign Office disingenuously called them, were seventy-nine lightly armed Royal Marines, supported by the small part-time volunteer Falkland Islands Defence Force, civilians with a modicum of military training. Not much to repel a fast-approaching Argentine armada with 10,000 troops and armoured vehicles, supported by 200 warplanes massed on the mainland within striking range.

A second Foreign Office cable was no more helpful than the first: 'We are aware of your plans for the defence of the Seat of Government and resistance to any incursion. The conduct of any operation, of course, is entirely a matter for you and the forces under your command. But is there any additional guidance you wish to have about specific rules of engagement?'

In simple language, it meant 'you are on your own'. Rex Hunt called it 'cautious diplomatic language'. Others would call it passing the buck. Foreign Office fantasy phraseology was an inadequate substitute for military might.

In Buenos Aires, intense military activity fuelled invasion fervour. I witnessed raucous rejoicing for a long-cherished ambition, at last achieved but short-lived. The Falkland Islanders, facing danger, desecration and an uncertain future, did not know then that their nightmare would herald a new dawn of development and prosperity.

I had made a fact-finding tour of the Falklands in 1981, getting to know the people and the lay of the land, giving my reports a personal factual basis. I even landed from the sea at San Carlos, where the task force landed fifteen months later to liberate the Islands. And I visited peaceful farm settlements which later became battlegrounds.

2

ARGENTINA IN MELTDOWN

Buenos Aires demonstrations. Galtieri – villain to hero. United Nations peace call.

Rex Hunt paid tribute to the British Ambassador to the United Nations, Sir Anthony Parsons, who had a more practical, persuasive way with words than the terse-tongued cable compilers at the Foreign Office in London. He convinced the United Nations Security Council to pass a resolution calling on Argentina to withdraw its forces. I was in the Argentine Foreign Ministry where officials testily tossed the cable down for me to see. They were dismayed that the resolution was not vetoed by the Soviet Union, Argentina's biggest trading partner, with which relations had grown greatly. Ministers believed they had lost the diplomatic initiative to Britain while securing their military objective.

In Downing Street, Margaret Thatcher's husband, Dennis Thatcher, who prided himself on his geographical knowledge, asked, 'Where are they?' It was a fascinating footnote to momentous events. He reached for *The Times Atlas of the World* 'to find out where the bloody hell they were!' The Defence Secretary, John Nott, peered at a map to pinpoint the tiny dots in the South Atlantic, which his drastic cuts in naval strength had placed in mortal danger.

The fateful few days leading to invasion had been marked in London by ignorance then disbelief, and in Argentina by volatile changes of mood, which illustrated how the invasion changed sentiment towards the unpopular regime, and explains why the junta acted.

Four days previously, on Tuesday, 30 March, I witnessed violent public protest erupt into the biggest demonstration against the junta since the military seized power in 1976. Defying a ban on demonstrations, I joined thousands of protestors in Buenos Aires' main square, the Plaza de Mayo, trying to storm the Presidential Palace. Inside, General Galtieri nervously sipped his favourite tipple, Scotch whisky, the only habit he had in common with Margaret Thatcher. Unknown to the hostile mob outside, he had already given the order for the invasion. His army, navy and air force were mobilising and on the move.

The demonstrators were driven back by tear gas, water cannon, rubber bullets, and helmeted riot police charging on horseback with flailing batons. Holding my small radio to my ears, I was surrounded by riot police, thrusting their guns into my back and stomach, accusing me of directing the rioters by walkie-talkie radio. No, I told them, I was just listening to the *BBC Five O'Clock News*! Their sweating faces registered menacing disbelief.

I escaped to the telephone exchange to file my despatch, choking from tear gas. No one at the BBC or elsewhere took much notice of the violence erupting in Argentina. It was a side-show on the world stage.

The regime's crackdown on rioters was swift – 2,000 arrests in Buenos Aires and hundreds more in provincial cities. Others were wounded by rubber bullets and real bullets. Many were beaten up. The military rulers reminded them that demonstrations were banned under emergency regulations. The demonstrators denounced it as brutal repression, in what one newspaper called 'a day of rage'. Their cry was for justice and bread, an end to repression and human rights violations, and a return to democracy.

Two days later, the square was the venue for a different demonstration: the weekly Thursday gathering of the long-suffering human rights group 'Mothers of the Plaza de Mayo', demanding to know the fate of their missing children, mostly teenagers, at the hands of the regime. For more than four decades, the Mothers have demonstrated in silence in a mood of profound sadness, mourning their children who had disappeared without trace, victims of the very juntas with whom successive British governments had been negotiating to hand over the Falkland Islanders.

Fast forward twenty-four hours to the morning of the invasion, and the atmosphere had completely changed. The square was thronged with 250,000 demonstrators yelling their praise of Galtieri, shouting, 'Las Malvinas son Argentinas' ('The Falklands are Argentine'). It was an astonishing reversal of fortune for the junta, removing the threat of its immediate overthrow. The demonstrators threatened to beat me up. But the crowd formed a protective cordon around me, saying, 'Leave him alone. This is our day of celebration.'

As the warm sunshine bathed the square in light, the tall, uniformed figure of Galtieri emerged onto the balcony of the pink presidential palace, the Casa Rosada, a balcony made famous by Eva Perón, 'Evita', the iconic wife of former military President Juan Domingo Perón, who had renewed the sovereignty claim during the Second World War when Argentina supported Nazi Germany.

Galtieri smiled broadly and held his arms wide as if to embrace the multitude below, basking in their adulation, as he boasted of his capture of the Islands and barked his defiance of Britain.

The agony and the ecstasy of a fractured, tortured Argentina had been played out in those fateful four days. The faltering junta had saved itself briefly but had brought on its own demise.

In the next seventy-four days, the warm sunshine gave way to winter, as the savage South Atlantic storms swept up from the Antarctic. The atrocious weather would be a potent factor which almost scuppered the British task force in what its commander, Admiral Sir John 'Sandy' Woodward, and the land force commander, Major General Sir Jeremy Moore, called a 'close-run thing', echoing Wellington's famous comment on the Battle of Waterloo the previous century.

Throughout the day of the invasion the British government waited in vain for official confirmation. The Governor had hastily scribbled down the simple message: 'Invasion has started. Closing down.' The cypher equipment to encode messages was thrown into the harbour. But the transmission failed as a result of a technical glitch as the Cable and Wireless radio link switched the receiving station in the United Kingdom to frustrate Argentine attempts to jam messages. Ironically, it jammed the Governor's invasion message!

Thatcher promised Parliament that the Islands would be retrieved. 'We cannot allow the democratic rights of the Islanders to be denied by the territorial ambitions of Argentina … There will be no change in sovereignty without their consent.'

The Prime Minister who had once famously boasted 'the Lady is not for turning' (on her policies) had performed a complete U-turn. Only days earlier, her government was ready to hand over the Islands to one of the most brutal regimes in Latin America.

Thatcher said that if this kind of force was allowed to succeed, there would be many other examples the world over. Someone, some country, had to say, 'Stop.'

The Foreign Secretary, Lord Carrington, a man of principle, resigned, taking the blame for diplomatic failure, along with his two deputy ministers, Humphrey Atkins and Richard Luce. Lord Carrington's distinguished political career was over, having first been a minister in Churchill's post-war government. Fittingly, for a wartime officer decorated for gallantry, he became NATO Secretary General during the climax of the Cold War with the Soviet Union. He died in 2018, aged 99, widely respected for his integrity.

The small Royal Marines Falklands contingent resisted bravely, killing several Argentine invaders, but were ordered by the Governor to surrender to avoid bloodshed. The Argentines consolidated their occupation, pouring in troops, and occupied South Georgia 800 miles to the south-east, overcoming fierce resistance from a dozen Royal Marines landed from HMS *Endurance*. They killed three Argentine marines, destroyed a helicopter, and damaged a corvette.

The British diplomats flew out of Argentina, and there was an exodus of some Anglo-Argentine families from one of the biggest expatriate English and Welsh communities in the world, with descendants numbering about 250,000, many with dual nationality.

3

DOWNCAST DEFENCE SECRETARY, UPBEAT ADMIRAL

Intelligence warnings ignored. Ill-timed navy cuts. Action-man Admiral puts steel into Iron Lady. Task force sails.

The defeatist advice of Defence Secretary, John Nott, was that it was impossible to retake the Islands, faced with daunting logistics and Argentina's geographical advantage.

The hero of the hour suddenly appeared to reassure Margaret Thatcher – the First Sea Lord and Chief of the Naval Staff, Admiral Sir Henry Leach. A veteran of Second World War sea battles, he swept aside Nott's pessimistic portents and promised he could despatch a task force within two or three days to recapture the Islands. Ironically, John Nott had previously come close to sacking Admiral Leach for opposing Nott's 1981 navy cutbacks, which signalled the end of the task force concept of projecting power with a global reach. The cuts would slash the frigate fleet from fifty-nine to fifty and scrap other warships. Fortunately for Britain, these had not yet gone ahead. Britain's only ice patrol vessel, HMS *Endurance*, destined to be scrapped in March only days before the invasion, was on her last patrol in the South Atlantic, and two aircraft carriers, which had already been sold abroad, HMS *Hermes* and HMS *Invincible*, had not yet been delivered. All three ships were invaluable in winning the war. Though kept secret at the time, *Invincible* was hampered by engine breakdown.

Margaret Thatcher asked whether the task force could reach the Falklands in three days. 'No,' Admiral Leach told her. 'Three weeks. The distance is 8,000 nautical miles.' And would it be led by the aircraft carrier HMS *Ark Royal*? she asked. 'No,' replied Admiral Leach. The government had temporarily taken her out of service!

Nott was sceptical about the viability of such a risky operation. But Thatcher was convinced: 'Henry Leach had shown that if it came to a fight, the courage and professionalism of Britain's armed forces would win through.' Admiral Leach said: 'Faced with a crisis, we had a Prime Minister with courage, decision and action to match it.'

Sir Henry urged that they should not 'pussyfoot' with half-hearted measures but send 'every element of the fleet of any possible value. What is the use of a navy if you don't use it?' An armada of 199 ships and 20,000 men sailed south.

Admiral Leach was a man of action but few words in the Nelsonian tradition. His directive to go into battle had only nine words: 'The Fleet is to be made ready and sailed.' In his Northwood headquarters near London, the Commander-in-Chief of the Fleet, Admiral Sir John Fieldhouse, who was to oversee the whole campaign, codenamed Operation Corporate, asked for more time to prepare. Admiral Leach replied, 'No!' His prescience and professional preparedness made up for the politicians' prevarication. It was his last major act of a distinguished career. He died in 2011, aged 88, the unsung hero of the war.

The Prime Minister rejected a face-saving negotiation proposed by the Labour Party's leader, Michael Foot, to withdraw the fleet to avoid war. She had very little sleep but remarkable stamina as she presided over the War Cabinet, making life-and-death decisions. She emerged a heroine and won the next general election in 1983, her popularity restored by the 'Falklands factor'.

The real heroes were the task force and the Islanders. The military campaign which trumped Galtieri's failed gamble succeeded against all the odds and appalling winter weather. The resolve and courage of the armed forces, led by outstanding commanders, reversed flawed political policy and procrastination, naïve navy cutbacks, and dubious diplomacy.

4

ARGENTINA'S 1983 DEADLINE

Argentine deadline puzzles Thatcher.
Prime Minister and Defence Secretary 'culpable'.

The junta occupied the Falklands in the year they had vowed to do so, before its publicly-declared deadline, January 1983. This marked the 150th anniversary of what they describe as 'the expulsion of an Argentine population from the Islands' in 1833 by a British naval captain, who had been sent there to restore order. Argentina's inaccurate account of this incident festered in Argentine minds for 150 years, sowing the seeds of the dispute.

New research on this historically significant event rejects the Argentine account as untrue and discredits its sovereignty claim. The British captain did not expel a resident Argentine population, but only a mutinous garrison that had murdered its own commanders.

The invasion may not have been such a surprise if British governments had read the history books and heeded warnings from their own intelligence service over several years. Instead, they engaged in years of ineffectual negotiations and appeasement policies to hand over the Falkland Islands voluntarily.

The Argentine junta acted impulsively in a mood of opportunism to avert its own imminent collapse amid violent domestic dissent, economic failure, corruption and repression.

The junta cynically turned its population's anger into support for precipitate implementation of a nationalistic ambition to acquire 'Las Malvinas', their name for the Falkland Islands. It was an obsession nurtured by 150 years of falsehoods and distortion, still propagated today in schools and in its modern multimillion-dollar 'Malvinas Museum', to which thousands of pupils are taken by bus every week. Argentina lost the war but never ceased its unremitting propaganda campaign.

5

COUNTDOWN TO CONFLICT

Scrapping Falklands guard ship sends wrong signal.

For years, the Ministry of Defence (MoD) had refused to send reinforcements to the Falklands. The MoD said it would be a 'practical nonsense to attempt serious operations against a perfectly competent and well-equipped local opponent off the toe of South America'. It was costly advice which the Royal Navy would prove to be wrong.

Lord Carrington opposed the Defence Secretary's decision to axe HMS *Endurance,* the designated Falklands guard ship and the navy's only strengthened ice patrol vessel. Carrington thought it was 'the wrong signal', suggesting lack of commitment to defend the Falklands.

Nott argued that *Endurance* (launched in 1962) was old and expensive to maintain with no defensive role. Thatcher backed him, saying the ship had limited military capability. Parliament's Foreign Affairs Committee, as detailed in Freedman's history, later criticised her as being 'either ignorant of the ship's political significance or chose to ignore it'. In fact, *Endurance* was equipped with sixteen missiles, two helicopters, two deck guns, and sophisticated listening devices manned by Spanish-speaking technicians, to intercept Argentine intelligence signals twenty-four hours a day, a vital asset in the run-up to the invasion.

Endurance maintained the UK's presence in the Antarctic, affectionately known to scientists of all nations there as 'the Red Plum' with her red-painted hull colourfully contrasting with the white ice environment. Only six weeks before the invasion, Lord Carrington unsuccessfully urged Nott to change his mind. However, Nott was dissuaded from disposing of two troop-carrying ships, *Intrepid* and *Fearless*, which were indispensable in the conflict to come.

James Callaghan, who served in the Royal Navy in the Second World War, warned that the withdrawal of *Endurance* would have 'serious consequences'. Five years earlier, as Prime Minister during heightened tension in 1977, he had sent a submarine and other naval units to the South Atlantic as a deterrent. Official post-conflict inquests expressed surprise that similar measures were not taken in early 1982.

Remarkably, three decades before the invasion, Winston Churchill, with his renowned prescience perfected in two world wars, took similar deterrent action. In 1953 and 1954, he vetoed the sale of dozens of British helicopters which Argentina said it wanted for navy communications, air-sea rescue and crop-spraying. Churchill sent a crack Royal Marines unit to remove an Argentine naval encampment on the British South Sandwich Islands, where Argentina again established a naval camp in 1976. In 1954, Churchill's military chiefs told him that Argentina could seize the Falklands without difficulty.

Forty years earlier, as First Lord of the Admiralty at the start of the 1914 war, Churchill sent a fleet to the Falklands to defeat and destroy a German naval force attempting to seize the Islands. Unlike Margaret Thatcher, he knew exactly where they were and recognised their strategic value and their convenient location as a gateway to the Antarctic.

Only a few weeks before the 1982 invasion, negotiations were intensified to cede Falklands sovereignty to Argentina. Foreign Office minister Nicholas Ridley and his predecessors spent years striving relentlessly to get rid of the Falklands and to persuade the Islanders, according to the Foreign Office, that it would be a 'better life' than surviving in a 'stagnating economy'.

A flawed Foreign Office plan, intelligence alerts ignored, destructive defence cuts, delusional dictators – it was a toxic recipe for disaster.

6

SECRET ARGENTINE LANDINGS, UK ARMS SALES

Argentine encroachment by stealth. UK arms sales to Argentina. Labour's 'share power' plan.

All the time, Argentine commanders were secretly plotting military occupation. An invasion plan was prepared in the 1960s, enthusiastically sponsored by none other than Captain Jorge Anaya, who was the most militant member of the invasion junta as head of the navy. This early plan involved a surprise landing on the Islands, removal of all the inhabitants to Uruguay, and their replacement with Argentine settlers. I was told this by the editor of the *Buenos Aires Herald*, Robert Cox, who heard this from his neighbour, a retired navy captain.

In 1970–73, Prime Minister Edward Heath negotiated communications and oil supply agreements under which Argentina supplied fuel oil through its state company, YPF, and the Argentine Air Force operated a weekly air service to the Islands called LADE (Líneas Aéreas del Estado), built an airstrip, and opened an office in Stanley, which was a perfect screen for gathering intelligence on Falklands geography, defences and personalities.

In 1974, Harold Wilson's Labour government secretly offered to share the Falkland Islands with Argentina in a condominium.

President Juan Domingo Perón was said to have reacted with 'euphoria'. Perón told a colleague: 'Once we get a foot on the Falklands, no one will remove us. Shortly afterwards sovereignty will belong to Argentina alone.'

The offer was abandoned when he died just twenty days later, and Britain did not trust his successor, his widow Isabel Perón.

The proposal involved flying both the British and Argentine flags, Spanish and English to be dual official languages, and alternating UK and Argentine governors. The aim was to 'create a favourable atmosphere in which the Islanders could develop according to their interests'. The UK were out of touch with the resistance of the Islanders.

Argentina's clandestine establishment of a military base on the isolated British island of Southern Thule in the South Sandwich Islands, 1,200 miles south-east of the Falklands, in 1976 was a provocative act detected by a helicopter from *Endurance*. The Foreign Office told Captain Nick Barker to keep the discovery secret to avoid 'upsetting' the Argentines in advance of a resumption of talks. Argentina rejected a private Foreign Office protest requesting removal of the base, saying it was part of its navy's 'scientific programme'. The UK took no further action. How different from Churchill's decisive reaction more than thirty years earlier!

Southern Thule was the kind of territory the Labour Foreign Secretary Anthony Crosland favoured giving to Argentina as part of a compromise. It also fitted precisely the scenario that Argentine Admiral Juan José Lombardo revealed to me after the conflict – that Argentina's long-term plan, codenamed Project Alpha, was to continue to occupy isolated British islands so long as there was no British reaction. He mischievously described the South Sandwich landing as the 'first bite of the sandwich'!

At this time, the then head of the Argentine navy, Admiral Emilio Massera, ordered planning for the 'forcible occupation' of the Falkland Islands. Removal of the Argentine military from Southern Thule may have deterred the invasion. Ten years earlier, in 1966, tactical divers were landed from an Argentine submarine on the Falklands for covert reconnaissance of landing sites.

The Labour government, influenced by the Deputy Foreign Secretary, Alun (later Lord) Chalfont, who favoured transfer of sovereignty, agreed in 1979 to sell naval equipment, helicopters and missiles to Argentina. They even contemplated selling a destroyer and an amphibious assault ship, but these were ruled out, as were mortars and ammunition and 'any weapons that could be used either for internal repression [in which the dictatorship was intensively engaged] or to threaten the Falkland Islands [which the junta intended]'.

The Foreign Office had no objection to some arms sales to a regime whose human rights record was worse than that of Chile – on which the United Kingdom did impose an arms embargo, and which later gave the UK invaluable help during the 1982 conflict. Government critics called the weapons sales to Argentina 'reckless, odious and illegitimate'.

The Thatcher government went further and relaxed restrictions on arms sales. It was not only arms Britain was offering. A British trade minister, Peter Walker, on a visit to Buenos Aires before the invasion, enthusiastically outlined to me his plan for exchanging Scottish bull semen for Argentine Cox apples! I listened in disbelief. Argentina did not need bull semen, already having 40,000 cattle happily multiplying on its vast pampas grasslands. And English orchards were laden with Cox apples. What Argentina wanted were weapons of war, and the UK readily provided them, financed by a UK loan of £45 million which was never repaid. So, Argentina got, for free, weapons that would later be used against British forces in the Falklands conflict.

The Thatcher government upgraded diplomatic representation to ambassador level and chose an ambassador supportive of Argentina. A senior Foreign Office official, John Ure, visited Buenos Aires, where he advocated naval collaboration in the South Atlantic! The Ministry of Defence arms sales department suggested it might 'make sense' to sell Argentina an aircraft carrier, such as *Invincible* or *Hermes*, with Harriers! There was even discussion of selling battle tanks and Vulcan bombers, later used by Britain to bomb Stanley. But these sales were vetoed by the Foreign Office.

The head of the Argentine Naval Mission in London, Admiral Gualter Allara, asked to visit *Invincible* to watch Sea Harriers. The same Admiral later commanded the aircraft carrier deployed to sink *Invincible*. Britain had sold *Invincible* to Australia and *Hermes* to India, sales hastily cancelled when the carriers were needed as the vital core of the task force.

Because Argentina was regarded as a 'friend', British intelligence had failed to analyse its military capability, its forces, and its weapons. The invasion sent intelligence officers frantically consulting military magazines and manuals such as *Jane's Fighting Ships* and the Strategic Defence Review to determine what the task force was up against. BBC television correspondent Brian Hanrahan told me that on the long voyage south, British commanders were listening to my Buenos Aires despatches to glean any military information. They did not know that every time I got near any military bases, I was marched away by armed guards.

7

DUPLICITOUS DIPLOMACY, DELIBERATE DECEIT

Lying excuses for 'secret, deniable talks': 'Gone fishing, gone painting, private family holiday'.

The Argentine invasion followed nearly twenty years of subterfuge by the United Kingdom to hide from Falkland Islanders secret deals they were negotiating to transfer sovereignty to a murderous dictatorship, threatening the Islanders' livelihood and perhaps their lives. As they demonstrated in their occupation of the Islands, Argentina had no intention of honouring safeguards insisted upon by Britain in the negotiations as 'paramount' to protect Islanders' British way of life. Argentina's negotiators enthusiastically joined in the clandestine conspiracy to conceal the negotiations. Islanders' approval was to be sought only *after* agreement was reached.

All this was revealed by the military historian Professor Lawrence Freedman in his government-backed comprehensive review of the war. British ministers, his inquiry declares, indulged in 'deliberate deceit' in efforts to overcome the Islanders' resistance to their handover.

Foreign Office ministers tried to persuade the Islanders that it was in their best interests to become part of Argentina, despite its political and economic instability, human rights crimes, and a reign of terror, of which the British government was fully aware, as were we all in Argentina.

President Galtieri had managed the rare feat of currying favour with both the Soviet Union and the United States, whose ally he was in the US campaign against communist advance in Central America.

Three dangerous years in Argentina, reporting on the dictatorship in what was called 'the Dirty War', convinced me that both Conservative and Labour governments were guilty of naiveté, hypocrisy and delusionary policies, as events subsequently confirmed.

It is astonishing that successive UK governments made so many mistakes in encouraging an untrustworthy dictatorship, even to the extent of selling it weapons right up to the time of invasion and contemplating the supply of even more destructive equipment. It amounted to an invitation to the dictators to help themselves to UK territory and giving them the weapons to do so.

My despatches about Argentine repression brought me death threats and harassment from the kidnap squads who stalked me in the streets. My critical reports also made me unpopular with the British Embassy, whose lack of co-operation, I suspect, was dictated by the UK's devious diplomacy.

I was astonished to receive a telephone call several months before the invasion from the embassy's Argentine press officer, complaining that the diplomats kept her in the dark. Would I explain British policy to her? I told her they also kept me in the dark.

An April 1980 meeting between the Argentines and Nicholas Ridley in New York failed to agree co-operation on fishing, oil exploitation and improved communications. The Islanders' representative, Legislative Councillor Adrian Monk, a tough-talking farmer and anti-Argentine critic, was refused access to the briefing notes, with the excuse that he did not have security clearance! He opposed any Argentine presence in the Islands.

The Foreign Office said Ridley's 'personal relationship of confidence' was crucial in shifting Islanders from 'primitive antipathy' to the Argentines and 'chronic suspicion' of the British government. In fact, Ridley's abrasive manner alienated the Islanders. He practised the dark arts of duplicity, intrigue and subterfuge, whereas I found the Islanders to be straightforward, honest and pragmatic, and justifiably suspicious.

Ridley's duplicity was matched by Argentina, all the time working secretly on its invasion plan even as talks went on. Lying excuses were concocted to conceal the meetings, as detailed in Professor Freedman's history. Ridley suggested to Argentina's negotiator, Deputy Foreign Minister Air Force Comodoro Carlos Cavandoli, that they meet informally 'while fishing together on a Scottish river bank'. Instead, they chose an isolated venue in a picturesque Swiss village at Lake Geneva, in the Hotel du Lac. The cover story was that 'Mr Ridley was on holiday with his wife to do a little watercolour painting'. Ridley was 'to arrange his own bookings and pay the invoice himself'. If the meeting became public, a 'defensive' news briefing would say Mr and Mrs Ridley were on a private holiday and meeting Cavandoli was a 'social occasion', and the Foreign Office did not know what they talked about. This subterfuge was more far-fetched than cloak-and-dagger crime fiction. For the unsuspecting Islanders, their way of life was at stake.

Lord Carrington described Ridley's operation as 'hole in the corner' and 'furtive' and the cover story 'very thin', Freedman revealed. Governor Hunt was informed by letter, which he was ordered to destroy to avoid arousing speculation.

The Lord Chancellor, Lord Hailsham, expressed doubts about handing over British subjects to the 'whims and changes of a South American dictatorship'. These misgivings were set aside in

Britain's decision to avoid the heavy costs of a 'Fortress Falklands' or of economic stagnation in the Islands. It was argued that political settlement could unlock the economic potential of the region. But for whose benefit?

Ridley and Cavandoli were sworn to secrecy about their talks. They hatched a plan for the transfer of titular sovereignty to Argentina, with a ninety-nine-year lease-back for the Islanders to continue their 'way of life under British institutions, laws and practices'. But lease-back was subject to review every five or ten years, as Argentina wanted total control much sooner.

The plan, refining previous proposals, provided for the British and Argentine flags to fly side by side. The British Governor, with a locally elected council, would administer the Islands jointly with an Argentine Commissioner General. A joint council would co-operate on economic development, fishing, exploitation of oil, and Argentina would provide finance for developing the economy, even though its own economy was in chronic crisis with soaring inflation and shortages of essential items such as telephones. These proposals betraying the Islanders were close to fruition but aborted by the invasion.

Ridley was getting on famously with Cavandoli, who, Freedman reported, was 'bubbling with pleasure' over Ridley's company. This light-hearted camaraderie was out of tune with their deadly mission.

Cavandoli argued that Argentines should be allowed to buy or rent land and show how farming techniques could be improved, and he wanted the small Royal Marines detachment withdrawn.

8

ISLANDERS REBUFF UNREPENTANT MINISTER

'Keep Falklands British.' Ridley assailed by Parliament. Whose ostrich heads buried in the sand?

Ridley was desperate to get Islander support for the lease-back agreement, which he wanted not to be on the agenda but somehow, as explained in Freedman's history, 'to emerge spontaneously from the Islanders' deliberations as if it was their own idea'. The Foreign Office told Ridley to paint a grim picture of the alternatives of economic decline and Argentine aggression to make Falklands 'Councillors' flesh creep'. He had to avoid accusations of conspiracy and keep secret his progress with Cavandoli. But the Islanders were not fooled. They suspected he had already done a deal. One doughty Falklands champion, pub landlady Velma Malcolm, astute and knowledgeable as chairman of the Falkland Islands Association Stanley Committee, demonstrated that the Islanders were not, as the foreign office regarded them, 'As ignorant as sheep,' as she wrote in her book of that title.

Ridley travelled to the Falklands through Buenos Aires, where he had a 'quiet drink' with Cavandoli and presented him with a gift of a silver spoon for his newly born grandson. Ridley urged the Argentines not to be 'nice to him in public' but maintain antagonism and complain about 'lack of progress'.

Landing in Stanley on 22 November 1980, Ridley was greeted with posters declaring 'Keep the Falkland Islands British'. Meeting 400 Islanders in Stanley Town Hall, Ridley curtly rejected their objections.

There was deep distrust of Argentine promises and resentment that the UK government would not guarantee, if all went wrong, that all Islanders would be granted the right to settle in Britain with automatic citizenship.

Ridley's mission was denounced by the London lobby support group, the Falkland Islands Committee (later to become the Falkland Islands Association), and in Parliament by members of all main parties.

Governor Hunt said the Islanders could not be manipulated. They had survived for 150 years and could survive another 150 years without concessions to Argentina.

The Foreign Office disagreed with Hunt that the Islands could be viable without close links with Argentina, and there could not be alternative air and sea services if Argentina cut communications. The Treasury warned that Britain could not afford the £6 million to replace them. It was, in retrospect, a miniscule amount. Hunt was right and the Foreign Office wrong, as post-conflict progress proved.

Prophesies of doom persisted. Ambassador Anthony Williams said the Islanders could not continue to use facilities provided by Argentina – such as the air service, supplies of fuel, food and other freight – while 'insulting' the Argentines. He wanted to visit the Islands 'to instil fear in them of the consequences'. He was criticised by the Islanders for appeasement. Lord Carrington told me the above, and that Williams's support for Argentina by withholding vital information from him was unforgivable. Argentina exerted pressure by altering or cancelling flights to the Islands, impeding passengers, mail, food and fuel.

The Foreign Office described the Islanders as 'ostriches with their heads in the sand'. It thought Ridley's visit had 'pulled Islanders' heads out of the sand' and every effort had to be made to 'counter their understandable inclination to bury them again'. Events showed it was the ostrich-like British government that did not see the invasion coming. The Foreign Office's insulting references to the Islanders did not become public until much later.

The Islanders had their heads not buried in the sand but held high, focused on the tyrannical regime over the horizon. A Falklands legislator, John Cheek, summed up their sentiments to me: 'There is no Argentine government we would accept or trust. Most Islanders would rather emigrate to New Zealand.'

After the conflict, Ridley, blunt as ever, told me: 'If the Islanders had agreed my plan [on lease-back] nearly one thousand people would not have been killed in the war.' What he did not acknowledge was that their defeat brought down the military junta, prevented Argentina's planned invasion of Chile, liberated the Islanders, and ended repression and mass murder of Argentina's own citizens.

I interviewed Ridley in Belize, where the UK pursued a policy perversely opposite to that in the Falklands. Both as a British colony and after its independence in 1981 as a Commonwealth country, Belize was defended by 1,500 British troops, and Harrier aircraft, to deter invasion by Guatemala in furtherance of its sovereignty claim to a British territory. I joined British forces dug in on the border to repel Guatemala's large army and confront a military regime as ruthless as Argentina's. The UK attitude was not appeasement, as with Argentina, but tough resistance. And it worked. Guatemala dropped its claim in 1992. A similar posture could have averted the Falklands invasion.

9

INVASION SPECULATION RIFE

Argentina in crisis. Soaring inflation, hunger and demands for democracy.

My BBC despatches, charting day-to-day attitudes, reported growing invasion speculation and how Argentina was dangerously unstable with a collapsing economy, wholesale murder by the death squads, a hardening attitude over the Falklands, and tensions over its territorial dispute with Chile.

On 20 December, I broadcast a despatch on 'Christmas death threats': I reported that death threats had been made to relatives of missing people and political prisoners in Christmas letters bearing a picture of a skeleton and an inscription saying '*Enjoy your last Happy Christmas*.' The threats were believed to be from the secret intelligence services, which had made similar death threats in the past – and carried them out.

My despatch on 12 January was headed 'Argentina in crisis':

Argentina has its third military president in one year. It is plunged deep in economic crisis. Its people are restive. Many are out of work. Some are hungry in one of the world's biggest grain-exporting and beef-eating countries. One newspaper carries a stark one-word headline: 'Hunger'. In north-west Argentina alone, 400,000 children suffer chronic malnutrition. Many of them are in danger of dying. In a land of plenty it comes as a shock. Inflation is running at about 150 per cent. Its currency has been devalued 500 per cent in less than a year. They have introduced a 100-million-peso bank note. It is worth little more than £50. Argentina is one of the most cultured, best educated, richly-endowed nations on earth – and one of the worst-managed. Argentina is chronically unstable. During their six years in power, the Generals have ruthlessly wiped-out subversion and opposition. They have failed to account for thousands of people who have disappeared.

Yet the UK insisted the Islanders would be 'better off' under Argentine rule. How wrong can you be?

Despatch on 'Human rights protests', 21 January:

Argentina's five main political parties, whose activities have long been banned by the military regime, have launched a campaign of protest against the new (Galtieri) regime, demanding a return to civilian rule. The human rights campaign for information on the thousands who have disappeared, has also been intensified. General Galtieri faces growing opposition from the emboldened political parties and trade unions. They have denounced successive military governments since the coup of 1976 as failures.

Invasion speculation continued to grow, as I reported on 25 February 1982, five weeks before the invasion:

Speculation that Argentina's generals may resort to force in an attempt to invade the Falkland Islands to get their way is emphatically discounted by the Foreign Ministry. There is a temptation for military regimes to focus on a foreign issue of this kind, on which Argentine people are united, to divert their attention from divisive domestic issues. A Foreign Ministry spokesman told me Argentina's patience is running out and the new Galtieri government wants 'quick results' (on surrender of sovereignty). The Islanders don't want to be part of Argentina. They insist they are British and want to stay that way. They have rejected a British compromise proposal to surrender sovereignty and for lease-back of the Islands. This they regard as a dangerous move opening the way to complete Argentine takeover. The Argentines have promised to respect the interests of the Islanders and guarantee their lifestyle, traditions and democracy. The Islanders are understandably sceptical, pointing out that successive Argentine regimes have been unable to guarantee democracy in their own country.

The warning signs were so obvious and so public, I could not understand why the British government did not react.

The UK still insisted the Islanders would be 'better off' under Argentine rule. How wrong could it be? I wonder what messages were being relayed to London by the embassy, and what notice the FCO were taking. Lord Carrington told me he was misled by Ambassador Anthony Williams.

10

FALKLANDS CALM, ARGENTINE MAYHEM

Clash of cultures. Peaceful penguin paradise. Noisy, brash Buenos Aires.

The dispute involved a stark clash of cultures, language, and a differing perception of history, creating an unbridgeable gulf of incompatibility. Macho braggadocio generals in the humid heat of busy, bustling Buenos Aires were indulging in indiscriminate killing. The turmoil and mass agitation in Argentina was a world away from life in the Falklands, which had gone on at the same serene pace for a century-and-a-half of peaceful British rule.

A few days before the invasion, Rex Hunt, a former Royal Air Force Spitfire pilot, took to the skies in his private plane with his student son as his passenger. They flew over a rural landscape dotted with hamlets huddling around harbours and inlets. The clear, unpolluted waters and sandy beaches were home to a variety of wildlife and, beneath the surface, teeming with fish. It was a landscape of limitless horizons, with 600,000 sheep. The Islanders ate mutton so regularly they called it '365' for all the days of the year!

What a difference from the noisy, fume-filled, car-crazy Argentine capital with its skyscrapers, millions of people, thousands of revving horn-blowing buses, and colourful tango shows. Here it was not '365' mutton, but beef every day of the year.

They had as many cattle roaming the vast expanse of the pampas as they had people. Argentina enjoyed huge natural resources of all kinds: meat, grain, minerals and oil, as well as manufacturing industry and nuclear power stations fuelled by their massive deposits of natural uranium. They seemed to have everything except the one prize they coveted most ... the Malvinas. Yet I never met a single Argentine who wanted to live in the Falklands!

Much of the world knew little or nothing about the Falkland Islands. The invasion brought me many telephone calls asking what and where they were. So, I broadcast a comparison of life there and in Argentina on the long-running programme *From Our Own Correspondent*:

> The tranquillity of the Islands was far from the world's mainstream and that's how the Islanders wanted to stay. To them it did not seem much to ask. To Argentina's rulers it was an affront to their national pride. To Britain, it was a relic of Empire, once ironically a vital naval base, now an inconvenience, an embarrassment to better relations with Argentina. But the British government insisted the Islanders' wishes were paramount. And to Britain it is people who matter. To Argentina's military establishment, people are not so high in their order of priority, as they have so often ruthlessly demonstrated. Their human rights record is one of the worst in Latin America. You could not anywhere find such a yawning gap of incompatibility between two sets of people ... the Latin American military with its macho, iron fist approach ... and the simple lifestyle of the Falklanders – the shepherd alone on horseback except for his dogs and the sheep in the rain and the biting wind, his wife warming herself with the peat they dig themselves ... baking her own bread, sometimes teaching her own children in tiny farm schoolrooms. So often they tried to

explain to me why they loved the life so much … the peace, tranquillity, a place where delightfully robust, red-cheeked children
roam happily, and romp with the penguins without fear of harm
or molestation. Now one set of people are trying to impose such
an alien culture on the other. The Military Governor says there
will be changes, replacing English with Spanish, driving on the
right instead of the left, their colourful wildlife postage stamps,
sought after the world over by collectors, have given way to the
impersonal, ominous military rubber stamp. The Islanders have
been threatened with jail for showing 'disrespect' to the invaders
… a jail which until now hardly ever housed anyone except the
occasional harmless drunk. The Military Governor has promised
Islanders they will have the full rights of all Argentines under the
Argentine Constitution. He failed to mention it is a constitution
contemptuously cast aside by military rule, denying Argentines
themselves so many basic rights. What will the Argentines do with
what they call their lost lands? They tell me they do not want to
live there in the cold and the gales in the bleak South Atlantic.
Perhaps they want the oil believed to lie offshore or the fish that
teem in those same waters? The Argentines worship beef, not fish.
So, it comes down to obsessional nationalistic pride. The military
have launched a repetitious propaganda campaign to condition
the public's mind. Endlessly, snatches of television carry martial
music and pictures of the armed forces in action under the blue
and white national flag, warships, planes and troops shouting
'Si Juro! Si Juro!', Spanish for 'I swear', the traditional reply to
the Argentine military oath to swear to defend flag and country
and to die if need be. The martial music is getting monotonous.
Will that be enough to keep together a nation, already split by so
many deep divisions, in the gravity of armed conflict and perhaps
much bloodshed? The euphoria of invasion day and the epithets

'glory', 'patriotism', 'victory' is giving way to sombre realisation of the magnitude of what may lie ahead. Many Argentines, ordinary, decent, humane people, as so many are outside the military, have voiced their misgivings to me. Their views echo what one Argentine acquaintance said to me: 'El Presidente es loco!' [The President is mad]. He is a general who has never been to war. He does not know what he has done.

This eyewitness account is a snapshot in time giving an exact glimpse of life at that moment.

11

NEW JUNTA UPDATES INVASION PLAN

Galtieri seizes power. Navy Chief urges action. Junta demands speedy handover. Talks failure.

The British government should have been jerked into awareness of approaching danger when the new junta seized power
on 8 December 1981, led by Galtieri as Army Chief, along with
the Navy Commander, Admiral Jorge Anaya, and the Air Force
Chief, Brigadier Basilio Lami Dozo. Galtieri had overthrown his
ailing predecessor, General Roberto Viola.

The new junta updated its invasion plan and gave public
clues to its intentions. Galtieri appointed Dr Nicanor Costa
Méndez as Foreign Minister, a diplomat obsessed with seizing
Falklands sovereignty. Galtieri made a speech saying he wanted
to create a 'Greater Argentina', which, my Argentine contacts
told me, meant getting possession of the Falkland Islands and
the Beagle Channel islands from Chile. The UK failed to analyse the implications. Galtieri made no secret of Argentina's
priority for 1982 to resolve the Falklands dispute. The junta
reactivated negotiations even as they prepared to use military
force, timed for August, when the South Atlantic winter would
make it virtually impossible for Britain to recover the Islands.
By then, the UK might have delivered the aircraft carriers that
it had sold abroad

It would have been the perfect moment, but circumstances spiralling out of control meant they could not wait, as revealed by Admiral Anaya. He told a retired admiral on 19 December that the military government faced collapse and had to find an element 'to bring cohesion to the country and that element is the Malvinas'. His fellow admiral retorted that Margaret Thatcher would not be bullied. 'The British are like bulldogs. When they bite, they won't let go.'

On 22 December, Anaya sent a handwritten note marked 'secret' instructing Rear Admiral Juan José Lombardo to update the invasion plan, as Admiral Lombardo later told me. Lombardo, who commanded the South Atlantic operations, had a series of meetings with the head of Marine Special Forces who was to lead the invasion, Admiral Carlos Büsser, whom I also later interviewed.

Astonishingly, they met not in the security of their military headquarters but in full view of the public in the Florida Garden Coffee Bar in Buenos Aires's busiest tourist thoroughfare. They sat incognito in civilian attire, sipping their coffee as they scribbled refinements to the invasion plan in a school notebook in handwriting to ensure secrecy and avoid the risk of typewritten or carbon copies leaking. Not far away, victims of the regime were being tortured in a cellar. Admiral Büsser summoned a Marines Infantry Commander, Alfredo Weinstabl, on 29 January and handed him a piece of paper on which was written: 'Mission: To recover thee Malvinas and to restore it in perpetuity to the sovereignty of the Nation.' Training began for an amphibious landing.

On 27 January, Argentina demanded that negotiations be completed by January 1983, their publicly declared deadline. At talks in New York at the end of February, the Argentine delegation was led by its civilian Deputy Foreign Minister, Enrique Ros, and the UK delegation by Foreign Office Minister Richard Luce, who told me later that Ros seemed to have no authority to negotiate and kept referring back to Buenos Aires. That is no surprise when a military junta is calling the shots.

A joint communiqué talked of a 'cordial, positive spirit'. The junta angrily repudiated the joint communiqué on 2 March, demanding early transfer of sovereignty. Negotiation was over, and Plan B was activated – for invasion.

The Ministry of Defence had a Latin America Current Intelligence Group (CIG), which was given the impossible task of monitoring forty-six countries with only one squadron leader acting for all three services. In the MoD, one press clipping was flippantly annotated: 'Stand by your beds! Action stations will shortly be announced.'

Alarm bells should have been ringing loudly in London. Instead, it was judged that negotiations would continue. The government's Joint Intelligence Committee concluded no major military action was likely before the start of the southern summer in October. There was little sense of urgency.

But the Commander-in-Chief of the Fleet, Admiral Sir John Fieldhouse, worried about this inaction and wanted to reinforce the small Falklands Royal Marine contingent. The Royal Marines Commanding Officer in the Falklands in 1982, Major Mike Norman, asked how reinforcements might be sent in a crisis, and was cynically told: 'We'll parachute them in from Concorde.' As the South Georgia crisis deepened, Admiral Fieldhouse drew up his own contingency plan for Falklands action when the Foreign Office refused his plea to produce one.

After Argentina's truculent March communiqué, Margaret Thatcher, at last, ordered contingency plans be prepared for counter-action against Argentina. The MoD replied that effective military action is 'extremely limited' and would be 'too late and/or extremely expensive'.

SECTION TWO: WAR AT SEA, IN THE AIR, ON LAND

12

SOUTH GEORGIA IGNITES INVASION FUSE

Argentines land illegally, raise flag. Order to *Endurance* to remove them. Argentine military swamp Islands.

Confrontation came when an Argentine scrap merchant, Constantino Davidoff, landed on South Georgia with a contract confirmed by the British Embassy to salvage disused whaling stations that he had bought for £105,000. His workers went ashore from an Argentine naval ship without applying for a British permit to land. They provocatively raised the Argentine flag. The fifty-nine 'workers' included more military than civilians – thirty marines.

This was in line with Argentina's long-term strategy, 'Project Alpha', of stationing people on British territory, starting with Southern Thule. But the South Georgia landing did elicit a rapid British response – a warning to observe the entry formalities or the Argentines would be escorted off by Royal Marines from *Endurance*.

Argentina reacted sharply to what it regarded as an ultimatum and 'gunboat diplomacy'. It withdrew some of the men but left thirty-nine behind. The Argentine navy's plan was to establish a permanent military base in April after *Endurance* departed the South Atlantic on her final voyage.

To defuse an explosive situation, Carrington proposed sending a special representative to Buenos Aires, but Ambassador Anthony Williams objected, saying it would undermine his position. He told me he urged the Foreign Office to be placatory, delay action by *Endurance*, and avoid 'spectacular reaction … to trivial and low-level behaviour' which could cause lasting damage to Anglo–Argentine relations. As Lord Carrington suspected, Williams was acting not in British interests but in Argentina's. Urging a contrary course, Governor Hunt, his deputy Dick Barker, and Lord Buxton, a Falklands champion on a visit to the Islands, all advocated a tough response as Davidoff was no 'casual scrap merchant' motivated by commercial considerations but a front man in the naval campaign to create bases on British territory.

In a last-ditch compromise, Carrington sent a message to the Argentine Foreign Minister urging prudence, offering to cancel any forceful action so that the Argentines themselves could remove the workers. Belatedly, he was ready to speed up transfer of sovereignty. It was too late. The junta took the fateful decision on 26 March at 17:15 to invade the Falkland Islands. The UK still thought negotiations for peaceful handover were ongoing.

In retrospect, the junta had gambled too early. Another few weeks, as planned in their original timetable, and what was a virtually impossible task to liberate the Islands would have become definitely impossible. The junta had acted precipitately, motivated by rising domestic unrest against repression.

The invasion fleet sailed from Puerto Belgrano in the south on Sunday, 28 March. Even the units involved were not in the know. The operation was top secret, but such a large deployment should have been detected by satellite. The aim was to force Britain to negotiate sovereignty, not to fight a war. The UK reaction of sending a task force came as a shock to the junta.

The invasion demonstrated just how ill-prepared the Ministry of Defence was, helpless to reinforce the Islands. A Hercules transport aircraft could carry thirty lightly armed troops, but there was barely enough fuel at Stanley airport for its return flight. The runway was weak and could collapse under the weight of heavy aircraft. A greater force of paratroopers could not be sent because there were no in-flight refuelling facilities. Even Nott's dramatic suggestion to blow up Stanley airfield was impossible because the marines had no explosives!

Denied any options, ministers might well have asked what value they were getting for their defence budget of £13 billion a year! All they could do was despatch two nuclear-powered submarines, HMS *Spartan* and HMS *Splendid*, on 1 April. But they would take nearly two weeks to reach Falklands waters.

13

DIPLOMACY FAILS TO AVERT WAR

US dilemma: secret CIA plan to hand over Falklands to Argentina.

In March 1982, I got Admiralty permission to join *Endurance*, for her last visit to the Falklands. My news editor at the BBC queried why I wanted to 'bob about on an old boat in the South Atlantic' when I should be heading thousands of miles north to El Salvador in Central America to cover its elections.

Captain Nick Barker signalled that he could not pick me up in Montevideo because *Endurance* was stuck in South Georgia. The lone, vulnerable British warship, surrounded by hostile Argentine vessels, flashed a message of thanks to the BBC World Service in London, as I reported four days into the invasion:

6 April 1982: 'A report that *Endurance* had been sunk in the invasion of South Georgia has been denied ... A message to the BBC confirms that she is still there and her crew in good heart ... The message read: "The captain and ship's company congratulates and thanks you all at the BBC for your coverage. Your service is a great comfort to us all. HMS *Endurance* would like her best wishes transmitted to the British inhabitants of the Falklands and looks forward to another visit to Port Stanley."'

The BBC replied, sending warmest wishes to all on board HMS *Endurance* and relayed the ship's message to the Falkland Islands in its *Calling the Falklands* broadcasts, which were increased in the emergency from one a week to every day.

Diplomatic efforts to avert war were led by the United States, which publicly maintained an even-handed approach. Though the United Kingdom was its closest ally, the US did not want to alienate Argentina, its ally to counter communism in Central America. Argentina had sent troops to Nicaragua and El Salvador, experienced in repression and speaking the local language, Spanish.

Galtieri, who visited Washington a year before the invasion, came away convinced he could rely on the United States for support over the Falklands, not least from key officials, including Thomas Enders, responsible for Inter-American Affairs, and the US Ambassador to the United Nations, Mrs Jeane Kirkpatrick, who wanted the US to remain neutral to avoid alienating Latin America. The US National Security Adviser, Richard Allen, described Galtieri as 'a majestic charismatic personality'.

The Special Envoy for Latin American Affairs, retired General Vernon Walters, former Deputy Director of the Central Intelligence Agency (CIA), bluntly called it a 'silly dispute, a conflict of two egos, Leopoldo Galtieri and Margaret Thatcher', pointing out women seemed even more sensitive about their perceived machismo than men.

Galtieri was misled about US support. Thatcher had impressed Ronald Reagan even more. On the eve of invasion, President Reagan spent an hour on the telephone telling Galtieri that the UK would defeat Argentina and that the US would back Thatcher.

The American Secretary of State, General Alexander Haig, embarked on a marathon diplomatic shuttle between Washington, London and Buenos Aires. A plethora of peace plans, with contributions from the United Nations and Peru, failed. General Haig thought he would have rapport with the other generals. But he found Galtieri and his junta infuriating. Emerging from talks with them, he muttered to me: 'They are a gang of thugs and I don't know which thug is in charge! … I could never convince Galtieri that the British would fight back and win.'

A common theme in the peace proposals was military withdrawal by both sides, to allow talks on peace and the future status of the Falkland Islands.

A secret plan by the United States Central Intelligence Agency (CIA) proposed handing over the Falkland Islands completely to Argentina, paying the Islanders grants of $100,000 (£65,000) each to relocate to Scotland or some other British jurisdiction, or they could remain in the Islands to become Argentine citizens. The plan, disclosed in secret documents, was not declassified until 2017. It was hatched by the head of the CIA National Intelligence Council, Henry Rowen, who said he believed the grants would be 'sufficient inducement' to persuade the Islanders.

Knowing the Islanders as I do, they would never have contemplated any association or deal with Argentina, no matter how big the bribe. Money was not a consideration. For them, it was allegiance to the land they loved, pioneered and settled by their forbears over several generations. The grants would have been paid fifty-fifty by Britain and Argentina, which would also have paid compensation for damage caused by the invasion and for Island property they acquired. The CIA plan was never taken seriously. Britain had already committed its task force and the lives of its servicemen. The CIA thought the British had 'under-estimated' Argentine military capabilities and were unlikely to win a war 8,000 miles from home.

Reacting to the 2017 CIA disclosure, the Chairman of the Falklands Legislative Assembly, Dr Barry Elsby, said:

> The only opinion that mattered was that of Prime Minister Thatcher and the only people who 'underestimated' Her Majesty's Forces were the Argentine junta and, seemingly, the CIA. The idea that Islanders would give up their homes and way of life for money simply shows how little people under-stood the Islanders

A peace plan was proposed by Peru's President, Belaunde Terry, who asked me to mediate with Thatcher as I had previously interviewed both of them. I told him that as a mere journalist, I had no influence at that level. The Peruvian plan was rejected by Argentina on the same day as the cruiser *Belgrano* was sunk but that was not the reason for rejection, as my BBC despatch explained:

> It failed to satisfy the Argentine regime on its claim for sovereignty because it contained the condition that the wishes of the eighteen hundred Islanders should be taken into account which Argentina never conceded. Soon afterwards Argentina did say 'Yes' to a ceasefire proposal from the United Nations Secretary General but did not mention any concession on sovereignty or on withdrawal of their troops which the United Kingdom required.

My next despatch warned there were disadvantages for Britain:

> The sinking of the *Sheffield* creates a more favourable atmosphere in Buenos Aires for accepting a ceasefire on even terms instead of in a state of humiliation. A ceasefire at this stage could be to Argentina's advantage, leaving its troops for the time being on the Falklands, its claims to sovereignty intact, and the British fleet riding out the storms of the South Atlantic with the onset of winter. Time would be on Argentina's side.

14

FALKLANDS WAR A MISTAKE

Argentina poised to withdraw. 'War a mistake,' says Foreign Minister. US abandons mediation, offers UK arms.

Belatedly, Argentina was ready on 2 May to withdraw its troops, but Galtieri reversed his decision when Vulcan bombers and Harriers launched raids on Stanley airport.

In an exclusive interview never previously published, the Argentine Foreign Minister, Dr Costa Mendez, revealed to me what influenced Argentina's actions: 'We had no desire of fighting a war against Britain. The war was a mistake. The invasion was meant only to force negotiations.'

The Foreign Minister told me: 'General Galtieri said, "I think we should withdraw from the Islands" … the UN Security Council's resolution was what we wanted, a very compelling invitation to negotiate. But before withdrawing we wanted assurances that a resolution would be obtained by the end of the year.' (See appendix for full text.)

Galtieri decided again on 15 May to withdraw his troops, but faced too much opposition from the military in Argentina. Costa Mendez told me he first heard of the junta's invasion plans on 13 February 1982:

President Galtieri said that they were making military preparations … I was told on 26 March the invasion would take place … We thought that occupying the Islands would press Britain to negotiate or press the international organisations to intervene and try to obtain a peaceful end of the conflict.

The plan did not work because of the tremendous enthusiasm in Argentina. The government was a prisoner of its success. I was not free enough to negotiate the original plan which was to withdraw the troops and call for United Nations troops to occupy during the negotiations. Mrs Thatcher took too early the decision to send the fleet. That decision, given the tensions and general spirit in Argentina, provoked a harder, tougher attitude in Argentina.

My despatches described the public's enthusiasm for the invasion as I witnessed first-hand:

There has been an explosion of patriotic fervour and nationalistic pride as demonstrators took to the streets in their hundreds of thousands. A sea of blue and white Argentine flags waved above their heads as they chanted 'Argentina, Viva la Patria, Long live our country' and sang of victory and glory in century-old battle hymns from their struggle for independence from Spain.

The Argentines turned the Islands into a heavily armed fortress and prepared air raid precautions and civil defence on the mainland. They declared they would fight to the 'last soldier'. Some Argentine politicians feared the dispute might strengthen links with the Soviet Union, whose submarines might be sent to support Argentina against the task force. These fears did not materialise, but the Soviet Union did supply satellite information to Argentina on British deployments.

Four weeks into the conflict, on 1 May, the United States abandoned its mediation role and declared support for the United Kingdom, which the UK had expected at the outset. US government officials involved with Latin America were biased in favour of Argentina, but the US Defence Secretary, Caspar Weinberger, supported Britain from the outset, along with senior navy officers who had friends in the Royal Navy. Weinberger sidled up to the British Ambassador, Sir Nicholas Henderson, at a Washington reception and offered the United Kingdom use of a giant aircraft carrier. But Royal Navy personnel did not have the expertise to deploy it.

The US secretly supplied the UK with invaluable equipment, including shoulder-launched anti-aircraft Stinger missiles for the SAS (Special Air Service) and up-to-date Sidewinder missiles for the Harriers, enabling them to dominate the skies and disprove Argentine assertions that the Harriers were no match for their land-based Mirage warplanes. At the same time, Israel was sending arms to Argentina.

Ascension Island was the vital staging post and military base fortuitously located halfway between the UK and the Falklands, without which the campaign could not have been possible. It had been in Britain's possession since 1815, but control of the airfield had been given to the United States which immediately made it available. It became the busiest airfield in the world. Vast supplies of aviation fuel were tankered in by the US, which also provided invaluable satellite surveillance information.

As peace hopes faded, Britain, with submarines now on station, declared a 200-mile war zone around the Islands, warning that hostile forces could face attack. Argentina imposed a 200-mile war zone of its own around the Islands and the Argentine mainland, warning that all British aircraft and ships, including merchant and fishing vessels and civil airliners, would be considered hostile and treated accordingly.

Argentina introduced new austerity measures to fund the war, as I reported:

The measures include a big devaluation of the peso, nearly 17 per cent against the dollar following a cumulative devaluation last year of 500 per cent, petrol price increases of 30 per cent, a war tax on currency transactions, bigger taxes on cigarettes and tobacco, restrictions on imports and incentives to exports from Latin American countries supporting Argentina. All this will boost Argentina's already high inflation rate running at about 200 per cent. The aim is to prevent any further run on the country's already depleted foreign currency reserves and to boost exports in the face of trade restrictions imposed by the European Community and other countries. The public who have supported the sovereignty claim are being asked to make sacrifices to fund the war. South American countries are intensifying moves against British interests. Venezuela has suspended a multi-million-dollar deal to purchase military aircraft from Britain, and Peru announced a boycott of British ships, airliners and mail. War comes at a high price!

General Galtieri, with thirty-nine years' army service, depicted himself as a pragmatic man of action. 'I like simple words and clear ideas.' He had retained the dual role of Head of the Army as well as President to make his position more secure. But I was soon reporting it might not be secure enough as the economic cost of the war soared, causing more misery for the Argentine public:

Galtieri has met mounting criticism as rumour swept Buenos Aires that he was about to be deposed amid growing public unrest over the economic malaise and prolonged military rule. Many Argentines believe that the Falklands takeover was timed to defuse the powder-keg of domestic discontent and forge these restless forces into a unifying whole on the only issue this country could be united upon – the Falklands. It has worked – for the time being. The underlying problems could again burst to the surface once the immediate crisis and the overriding commitment to patriotism is over. On Falklands sovereignty, if not on the conduct of the conflict, it appears to be a strong regime with public backing. As a long-term feature of Argentine politics, military rule is thought to have little future. Galtieri fancies himself as a military ruler who could turn into an elected populist president as head of a new political party linked to the armed forces. But the challenge of the old parties remains, especially Peronism, the potent partnership between right-wing dictatorships, the workers and the poor. The ghosts of its creator, Colonel Juan Perón, who died nearly ten years before Galteiri's accession, and of his charismatic second wife, Evita, still haunt the generals, who fear a resurgence of Peronism most. This week many people went to a special Mass in several churches to mark Evita's birthday, thirty years after her death. The Peronists believe the Falklands conflict has strengthened their campaign for a return to civilian government and an end to military rule.

So it proved. Galtieri resigned within days of his defeat, and military rule ended a few months later. Argentina's suffering public, as well as the Falkland Islanders, were liberated by Britain's victory.

15

BELGRANO SUNK, HEAVY LOSS OF LIFE

Submarine torpedoes cruiser. Argentines concede it was a legitimate military target involved in pincer attack.

The first outbreak of fighting came in early May, with the bombing of Darwin and Stanley and warships shelling military targets. Argentina's only cruiser, *General Belgrano*, was torpedoed by the submarine HMS *Conqueror* on Sunday, 2 May, and 323 of her crew (of more than 1,000) died, the largest loss of life in any single act of the war. It dealt a devastating blow to the junta, destroyed navy morale and sent their ships scurrying back to the safety of mainland ports.

The initial explosion killed 200 men. Another 850 scrambled into rubber life rafts as the burning cruiser began to sink, battered by wind and waves.

The two escorting warships fled, leaving them to die. Other Argentine warships and a reconnaissance aircraft located and rescued survivors in the life rafts, but many perished from exposure. Casualties would have been far fewer if the *Belgrano* had been kept at battle readiness and her escorts had conducted immediate rescue operations. The cruiser was a former United States warship which survived the Japanese attack on Pearl Harbour during the Second World War.

The British regretted such heavy casualties, but the action may have saved lives in the long run on both sides because the Argentine navy withdrew and never gave battle as planned. The task force's chances of winning the war were much enhanced. The cruiser's captain, Hector Bonzo, gave a news conference in Buenos Aires, which I attended:

> In a graphic account of the dying moments of the cruiser, sunk 36 miles outside the war zone declared by Britain, Captain Bonzo said the 44-year-old vessel was steaming slowly at only ten knots away from the war zone towards Argentina when two torpedoes struck. The impact of the explosions tore through four decks killing sailors in their dormitories and in the canteen. She sank within an hour. They never hauled down the Argentine flag flying at the stern which was the last they saw of the vessel as stern slid below the surface. 'Our flag,' the captain said, 'still flies at the bottom of the South Atlantic.' He told of a disciplined evacuation into life rafts to become victims of the Atlantic gales with 75-mile-an-hour winds whipping up waves 25 feet high and temperatures way below freezing. Men huddled together in covered life rafts to stay alive with their combined body heat but some life rafts had only three or four men in them who had to spread out to keep the rafts balanced and stop them overturning. Some of them froze to death on the rubber floor. Five days after the sinking the rescue operation goes on.

Conqueror's commander, Captain Christopher Wreford Brown, whom I interviewed later on San Carlos beach, impressed me as an ultimate professional, pragmatic and highly trained. He gave me a fascinating account of how he stalked his target.

He spent two hours working into an attack position in daylight. But visibility was only 2,000 yards at times. At periscope depth at slow speed, the submarine trailed behind, so she dived deeper to catch up. *Belgrano* was zigzagging but not using sonar to detect the submarine. Twice *Belgrano* moved out of range, but she was eventually attacked from 1,400 yards away.

Captain Wreford-Brown sent a brief signal to fleet headquarters at Northwood: 'Successfully attacked *Belgrano*. Two hits with Mark Eights. Evaded to East.' Mark 8 torpedoes, like *Belgrano* herself, were Second World War vintage. Unlike the more modern Tigerfish, this weapon could more easily penetrate the cruiser's heavy armour and anti-torpedo reinforcement. Another torpedo from *Conqueror* struck one of *Belgrano*'s escorting destroyers, *Bouchard*, failing to detonate but damaging radar, sonar and engines.

A reconnaissance aircraft was requested to provide anti-submarine cover and destroy *Conqueror*, who had sped away to evade depth charges fired by the destroyers. *Conqueror* was ordered from London not to attack any rescue ships. This humanitarian attitude was hardly echoed in the jingoistic triumphalism of *The Sun* newspaper's splash headline 'Gotcha', which sat brutally alongside the intense sadness of the young sailors' mothers I interviewed in Buenos Aires. Commander Wreford-Brown was praised for his professional conduct. Under navy rules of engagement, he had to carry out the order to attack or face court-martial.

The Argentine Congress called it 'a war crime' for which Margaret Thatcher should face trial in an international court. This demand was dismissed as unjustified even by Argentina's admirals and *Belgrano*'s captain. They conceded that the cruiser was a legitimate target and threat, and her sinking was militarily justified. The *Belgrano*, with her powerful long-range guns, was tasked with other warships to inflict what could have been devastating damage and almost certainly a fatal blow to the task force.

Conspiracy theories that the aim was to frustrate peace negotiations were denied by Britain. Controversy was aroused because the cruiser was outside the British 200-mile exclusion zone, but secret papers divulged thirty years later in 2012 prove that the *Belgrano* had been ordered into the exclusion zone. Major David Thorp, a signals intelligence expert who headed a top-secret signals interception unit on HMS *Intrepid,* said they intercepted a message from naval headquarters ordering the *Belgrano* and her escorts to a position *inside* the exclusion zone and not back to Argentina. In his book *The Silent Listener*, Major Thorp wrote that Thatcher ordered that his findings be kept secret to avoid disclosing Britain's eavesdropping capabilities.

The UK government had publicly warned the Argentine government on 23 April, nine days before *Belgrano* was torpedoed, that Argentine vessels, whether inside or outside the exclusion zone, might be attacked if they were a threat to the task force. British commanders were correct in assuming that the Argentine fleet was engaged in a menacing pincer movement led by the aircraft carrier *Veinte Cinco de Mayo* closing in from the north-west and the *Belgrano* from the south-east. The Argentine aircraft carrier would also have been sunk if detected by British submarines.

Argentina later confirmed that both of its battle groups had previously been advancing at full speed towards the conflict zone. But after the fleet commander, Rear Admiral Gaulter Allara, had analysed the risk of such an attack, the Commander of the South Atlantic Theatre, Admiral Lombardo, who had previously ordered the pincer movement, sent this intriguing signal in code: 'Withdraw from Luis to Miguel.' This was an order to the

Belgrano and her escorts to withdraw to shallower water to avoid nuclear-powered submarines, which cannot easily manoeuvre at shallower depths.

Twenty-two years later, in 2004, secret Argentine documents confirmed that the cruiser and her destroyer escorts were involved in a double-pronged action commanded by Rear Admiral Allara. His mission was to attack when favourable conditions allowed. On 2 May, the same day as *Belgrano* was sunk, Allara ordered an air attack on eight British ships which had been detected, but his attack was frustrated by bad light and lack of wind, normally so strong and persistent in the South Atlantic. This prevented the deadly, heavily laden fighter-bombers from taking off from the carrier's flight deck. The unpredictable weather sometimes frustrated the Argentines but not as much as it did the British.

Admiral Allara said: 'Although in my country and abroad, many voices condemned that action [of sinking *Belgrano*] from a strictly professional point of view, I cannot criticise it. She was a ship on a war mission. But the sinking diminished the chance of success of peace negotiations.'

This was disputed by the Chief of Defence Staff and member of Margaret Thatcher's War Cabinet, Admiral Sir Terence Lewin. He declared to me: 'There was never any doubt that this was the right political and military thing to do. It was not until after the cruiser was sunk that we knew anything of the Peruvian peace initiative which any way was a half-baked proposal which never had any chance of success.' As Foreign Minister Costa Mendez told me, it was the Harrier and Vulcan attacks on Stanley airport which scuppered the peace efforts.

Argentine civilians began showing resentment towards the junta and told me it destroyed the myth of the invincibility of the armed forces fostered by military and media propaganda.

16

ENTER EXOCET, EXIT HMS *SHEFFIELD*

Deadly Exocet missile sinks destroyer. Daring plan to infiltrate base to destroy Exocets and aircraft fails.

Anticipating revenge counter-attacks, Admiral Woodward ordered two warships bombarding Stanley to withdraw to safer waters. It was a wise move. Argentina struck back by sinking the destroyer *Sheffield* with a devastating weapon. My despatch gave the Argentine version of the attack:

> It was carried out by three modern French-built Super Etendard fighter-bombers armed with Exocet missiles. Two of the pilots said they had each fired a missile and each claim they hit a target, and one of the ships was bigger than the other. The sinking of *Sheffield* has given the military fresh confidence in their ability to strike back. They regard it as confirmation that their land-based aircraft would prove a formidable factor in the balance of forces. It was a day dominated by the sound of war which drowned out the more muted peace moves.

Admiral Woodward had identified the Étendards and Exocets as the main air threat to the task force. It was very difficult to detect and deflect the missile, launched from low level more than 20 miles away, skimming the waves to home rapidly onto its target.

The Exocet attacks were initiated from their Rio Grande air-base in the far south. *Sheffield*, one of three destroyers guarding the main British force from air attack, was caught unawares and unprepared, unlike her sister ship, *Glasgow*, captained by Paul Hoddinott, which was on full alert. *Glasgow*'s radar detected the approaching Étendards and took countermeasures, firing anti-missile chaff into the air. *Glasgow* sent out an urgent radio warning. But *Sheffield*'s receivers were not working effectively and did not receive it. Her radar failed to detect the attack because her satellite communications were transmitting messages.

Four of *Sheffield*'s anti-air warfare team of eight were out of the war room. One Exocet missile tore a gaping hole in *Sheffield*'s starboard side. It did not explode but breached the ship's fire-fighting equipment, rendering it useless to extinguish rapidly spreading fires.

After the conflict, a parliamentary inquiry in London concluded that modern warship design uses many plastic and other combustible materials, which proved unsuitable in battle. Twenty of the 281 on board *Sheffield* were killed, and another twenty-six were injured. The survivors were ordered by the captain, Sam Salt, to abandon ship. Admiral Woodward said it was an expensive lesson, disastrously mishandled. The task force needed to be fully alert as the troopship liner *Canberra* and other ships sailed south. They were plum targets for air and submarine attack.

Argentine pilots claimed they had attacked *Invincible* on 30 May with an Exocet missile and bombs, setting the carrier ablaze, but this was untrue. Admiral Woodward kept the carriers out of harm's way, prompting jokes that they were nearer South Africa than Argentina. *Invincible* and *Hermes* were indispensable. If either carrier had suffered major damage, the campaign to liberate the Falklands would probably have had to be abandoned.

The Argentine High Command had decided to target *Hermes* or *Invincible* with their last remaining Exocet missile. But a new, more effective Sea Dart anti-air missile system with a faster computer had been installed in the destroyer *Exeter*, commanded by an expert warfare specialist, Captain Hugh Balfour. It saved about fifteen vital seconds in engagement time.

The Argentines launched their attack with two Étendards accompanied by four Skyhawks, carrying bombs. Their brief was to use the Exocet missile as their guide to the carrier while the Étendards turned back for home. They flew low to avoid radar detection. But they were detected by the destroyers *Cardiff* and *Exeter* and the frigate *Avenger*. The Exocet, fired from 21 miles' range, passed harmlessly between *Exeter* and *Avenger*. *Exeter*'s first Sea Dart destroyed the lead Skyhawk 5 miles away, and a second Skyhawk was brought down. The other two pilots pressed home their attack on *Avenger*, but their bombs missed.

A front-page picture, falsified by an artist in Argentine newspapers, purported to show *Invincible* burning fiercely although she was 20 miles from the action. Argentine newspapers reported many false 'victories' that never happened.

France had delivered five Étendards and Exocet missiles to Argentina only five months before the invasion, along with French technicians from manufacturer Aerospatiale to maintain them. But President François Mitterrand, who gave Thatcher invaluable support, blocked delivery of another nine Étendards and Exocet missiles. They would have been a devastating force, making the difference between victory and defeat. They would have been delivered in time if the Argentines had invaded several months later as originally planned.

Admiral Woodward was relieved that all five air-launched Exocets had been deployed, one of which sank the *Sheffield*, two sinking the Cunard container ship *Atlantic Conveyor*, and one missing *Invincible*. 'Each time,' Admiral Woodward said in his book, 'they let loose at the first radar blip they saw – three incompetent blunders which may very well have cost them the war.'

Several other land-based Exocets were delivered by Argentina to the Falklands by cargo plane or ship. One was launched from a flat-bed trailer on 12 June, severely damaging the destroyer HMS *Glamorgan*, killing thirteen crew. Two Exocets shipped in on a vessel marked as a hospital ship were detected by Islander Fred Clark, an aircraft engineer who had worked in France on Exocet production. In a dangerous pre-dawn recce in freezing weather to a banned military zone during curfew, he saw two Exocet missiles in a Stanley jetty shed. He was challenged by a sentry whose thick winter gloves prevented him from firing his rifle. Fred Clark placated the guard with a cigarette and made his escape. These missiles were never used.

John Nott launched a frantic worldwide campaign to thwart Argentina's attempts to acquire more Exocet missiles. Nott succeeded, helped by the intelligence services of Britain, France and other countries. France had sold 2,000 Exocets to twenty-six nations, but Argentina failed to acquire them, even on the black market at inflated prices.

SAS commandos planned a risky clandestine attack on the Rio Grande Exocet airbase, to be preceded by a dangerous reconnaissance flight, codenamed Operation Plum Duff. In a night operation, Captain Jeremy Black sailed *Invincible* dangerously close to the Argentine coast to launch a Sea King reconnaissance helicopter, codename ZA 290, for a flight at the extremity of its range, with three navy crew and eight SAS combat troops, led by an officer known only as Captain Andrew M.

Argentine radar detected the helicopter, which disembarked its SAS team at an isolated *estancia*, 20 miles (30 kilometres) from Rio Grande. The helicopter flew on to land on a beach near Punta Arenas in Chile. The crew set fire to it, escaped into the hills, and were repatriated by Chile.

A search by more than 1,000 Argentine marines around Rio Grande failed to find the SAS team who, beset by difficulties, had aborted their mission. The SAS team would later turn up in Chile, whose government, led by General Augusto Pinochet, secretly gave the UK incalculable help throughout the conflict.

The reconnaissance flight was intended to glean information for a bigger SAS force to crash land on the Rio Grande base in two Hercules aircraft and destroy the Étendards and Exocets and kill the pilots. It was codenamed Operation Mikado, but never went ahead, which was just as well as the base was so strongly defended, it may have turned into a suicide mission.

What British intelligence did not know, as Admiral Lombardo told me, is that the Étendard aircraft were towed away at night from the base and parked on civilian roads to thwart such an attack.

17

EPIC LONG-RANGE BOMBER RAIDS

'Mission Impossible' boosts Islander morale. Argentine front-line fighter aircraft withdrawn to defend mainland.

The most spectacular and complicated exploits of the war were the Vulcan bomber raids on Stanley airport beginning on 1 May. These were the only combat missions in the long history of the delta-winged bomber deployed twenty years earlier as Britain's nuclear deterrent to Soviet nuclear attack. The Vulcan, nicknamed 'the Tin Triangle' by the crews, could also carry conventional bombs.

Codenamed Black Buck, the five Vulcan raids were the longest bombing missions ever made – a 6,760-mile (nearly 11,000 kilometres) round-trip from Ascension Island for the ageing aircraft. The bomb bays had to be hastily modified and the flight refuelling system and electronics updated.

More than a million gallons (5 million litres) of fuel were used in each mission. No fewer than thirteen Victor aircraft were deployed for air-to-air refuelling to get just one Vulcan to its target. With no intelligence on fighter and missile defence, the missions were carried out at night, in radio silence. The hazards multiplied and much went wrong. The lead Vulcan was forced to turn back when its cockpit decompression failed, threatening to freeze the crew to death. Technical failure forced one of the

Victor tankers to abort. Another tanker had a fuel leak, and one of the last two tankers broke its fuel probe in a violent tropical storm, leaving only one Victor to press on with the Vulcan, both acutely short of fuel and in danger of ditching.

The second Vulcan, piloted by Flight Lieutenant Martin Withers, flew on through a tropical storm, refuelling four times in flight. Despite blind navigation, lack of accurate maps, and detection by Argentine radar, it emerged from the cloud and miraculously spotted Stanley airport. Climbing to 10,000 feet, it dropped all twenty-one of its 1,000lb bombs. Only one was on target, creating a small crater towards the side of Stanley runway, which was quickly filled in.

The aircraft broke radio silence to signal the codeword *Superfuse*, indicating the raid had succeeded. The Vulcan got back to Ascension to complete its sixteen-hour mission. Catastrophe was averted when four of the refuelling Victors arrived back at Ascension almost simultaneously, desperately short of fuel, narrowly avoiding a pile-up on the crowded runway. This would have destroyed a quarter of the RAF's total South Atlantic tanker force.

Each Vulcan raid dropped twenty-one bombs, sixty-three in total. Only one hit the runway. All the other bombs fell harmlessly in the countryside. Only one radar-controlled gun was hit.

The mission, regarded by many as impossible, was conceived by the head of the RAF, Air Chief Marshal Sir Michael Beetham, a Second World War bomber pilot. He had commanded the Vulcan force and pioneered long-distance Vulcan refuelling with a flight from the UK to South Africa. He told the War Cabinet that the Vulcans' bombs could disable Stanley runway. In fact, damage was minimal, and the runway continued in use throughout the conflict. But the operational and psychological impact was enormous, demonstrating the RAF's long reach.

The explosions woke the startled Islanders from their sleep but boosted their morale. Islander Tony Chater recalled to me: 'The whole house shook, as though there had been an earthquake. There was terrific jubilation. From then on, we felt confident the British forces would come to our rescue.'

In Buenos Aires, incredulous members of the public, their fears heightened, asked me whether they were now a target for RAF bombs as well as submarine nuclear weapons. I told them the UK would not attack heavily populated civilian areas and that the task force submarines had no nuclear missiles.

The Vulcan mission was followed by Harriers from the aircraft carriers attacking anti-air installations at Stanley airport.

The Argentine air force had suffered a setback in the crucial air war. They redeployed their only dedicated Mirage fighter interceptor squadron from Rio Gallegos and Falklands operations, further north for mainland defence. Harriers could now intercept aircraft attacking the task force without interference from enemy fighters. The Vulcans had performed their first and last war mission. A surviving Vulcan stands silent sentinel outside its former base, RAF Waddington, a relic of the Cold War and of the longest air raid in history.

One of the navy's most successful Harrier aces, Commander Nigel Ward, was contemptuous of the Vulcan raids. He acknowledged the skill, endurance and bravery of the RAF pilots, but he regarded the operation as an unnecessary RAF intrusion into a predominantly naval, amphibious and land force campaign. Stanley airport could have been attacked more easily at much less cost by Sea Harriers and naval bombardment from 10 miles out to sea.

The Vulcan raids were phenomenally expensive, consuming fuel costing £500,000. Ward says the seven missions, some of them aborted, consumed enough fuel to fly 260 Sea Harrier bombing missions, dropping 1,300 bombs. The Vulcan raids used more than twice the fuel needed to support the 1,500 combat missions flown by the Sea Harriers during the whole conflict.

Commander Ward was an outstanding and courageous pilot. Canadian born, 'Sharkey' Ward had served twenty years in the Fleet Air Arm before he took on the crucial role of senior Sea Harrier adviser on the tactics, direction and progress of the air war, on which the defence and success of the task force largely depended. He was only 39.

It was a role for which he had the experience, leadership qualities, and flying skills by night and by day. He was an invaluable adviser as well as a front-line fighter ace and inspirational commander of 801 Naval Air Squadron on HMS *Invincible*. In more than sixty missions, he achieved three air-to-air kills and took part in or witnessed a total of ten kills.

He assembled two fighting squadrons flying from each carrier, just twenty Sea Harrier multi-role aircraft to take on more than 200 Argentine fighter and ground attack aircraft. Only six navy Sea Harriers were lost, all by accident or ground fire. A Harrier was shot down attacking Goose Green airfield, and two Harriers on patrol failed to return. This accident reduced by 10 per cent the task force air combat capability. In mid-May, they were reinforced by eight more Sea Harriers and six RAF Harriers. Not one was lost in air-to-air combat.

Admiral Leach said: 'Without the Sea Harriers there would have been no task force.' Nigel Ward wrote a bestselling book, *Sea Harrier over the Falklands*.

Flight Lieutenant Dave Morgan was one of the most effective RAF pilots, destroying several Argentine aircraft. Another outstanding pilot was to become professional head of the RAF as Chief of Air Staff.

Air Chief Marshal Sir Peter Squire was a wing commander on *Hermes*. His squadron of six Harriers flew a total of 151 sorties, mainly ground attack. Three RAF Harriers were brought down by enemy fire, and one crash-landed at San Carlos. Wing Commander Squire was in action daily over targets including Stanley airport, Mount Longdon and Dunnose Head airstrip, in which an Islander, Tim Miller, was blinded in one eye by shrapnel from an RAF bomb. Squire survived a crash-landing at Port San Carlos, and again when a missile exploded near his Harrier, and a bullet penetrated his cockpit. In another incident, engine failure forced him to eject before his aircraft crashed.

Air Chief Marshal Squire visited Argentina to meet the men he fought against, including General Walter Barbero, who, like Squire, became Air Force Chief. Squire explained to me that he told Barbero the British had great respect for the Argentine air force, their courage and skill. A helicopter pilot in the Falklands also became head of the RAF, Air Chief Marshal Sir Andrew Pulford.

RAF helicopters tirelessly ferried troops, supplies and casualties. The busiest aircraft of all was the lone Chinook helicopter (code-sign ZA 718 'Bravo November') which survived the sinking of the *Atlantic Conveyor* when three other Chinooks and other smaller Wessex helicopters were lost. In seventeen days of non-stop support of the land forces, the Chinook made an unrivalled contribution. It flew for 109 hours, carried 2,150 troops, including 95 casualties and 550 prisoners of war, and moved 550 tons of supplies. Its chief pilot was Squadron Leader Dick Langworthy.

18

BRITISH BACK
ON FALKLANDS

Secret advance SAS raids. Beachhead unopposed.

Elite special forces played a vital part in the conflict, arriving secretly long before the main landings. Special Air Service (SAS) and Special Boat Service (SBS) and Royal Marine Commandos, backed by HMS *Endurance*, led the assault to retake South Georgia on 26 April. A few days later, on 1 May, SAS and SBS patrols landed at night by helicopter on the Falkland Islands to reconnoitre enemy positions. They hid so skilfully that the farm manager at Port San Carlos, Alan Miller, told me he was unaware they were hiding for days in hedges close to his house. He was surprised when an officer popped up from behind a gorse bush and greeted him, 'Ah, good morning, Mr Miller.' Alan Miller's wife, back in the UK, had given the task force detailed local knowledge of the area.

Four-man patrols, heavily laden with equipment, were landed up to 20 miles from their objectives in open terrain with no trees for cover. They dug shallow hollows in the soggy ground, covering them with camouflaged chicken wire, moving only at night. They called in Harriers to destroy helicopters on the ground and attack a fuel and ammunition dump at Goose Green.

A daring SAS raid destroyed eleven Pucara ground attack aircraft parked on Pebble Island airstrip on 14 May, weakening Argentina's ability to attack British troops. The raid was led by Captain G. J. Hamilton, later killed in a gun battle near Port Howard on West Falkland. Brian Hanrahan, on a destroyer offshore, sent a BBC despatch describing the raid amid intense gunfire from the warships:

> The commandos touched down several miles from the target and took several hours to reach it across rugged country in the dark. In the dead of night, the battle exploded in front of me … From the sea the ships threw out orange flames and covering fire … salvo after salvo of high explosives, whining away into the darkness to land on the defenders, twenty at a time, one shell every two seconds, a tempo designed to terrify as much to destroy. A hundred shells were fired during the raid in little more than thirty minutes … The barrage was halted to prevent dropping shells onto Pebble Island settlement of about fifty people. The commandos moved in, blew up an ammunition dump and destroyed eleven aircraft, six of them Pucaras used for ground attack against troops.

The Pebble Island raid took place one week before the main landings at San Carlos on 21 May. Sixty SAS soldiers carried out diversionary attacks around Darwin and Goose Green air strip with small arms and mortar fire to prevent interference with the most vulnerable phase of the campaign, the amphibious landing of thousands of troops at night on beaches around San Carlos Water, on East Falkland. Codenamed 'Operation Sutton', the landings were successfully achieved under the command of Commodore Michael Clapp (Commodore, Amphibious Warfare), one of the three front-line leaders, along with Admiral Woodward and Brigadier Julian Thompson. They brilliantly masterminded the landings and most of the campaign at sea and on land, later co-ordinated by Major General Jeremy Moore of the Royal Marines. Their outstanding leadership was a vital factor in achieving victory.

More than 4,000 commandos and paratroopers forming 3 Commando Brigade, led by Brigadier Thompson, were put ashore with artillery and tanks at San Carlos (Blue Beach), Port San Carlos (Green Beach) and Ajax Bay (Red Beach). The landings were supervised by Major Ewen Southby-Tailyour, who had commanded the Falklands Marines detachment the previous year. As a keen sailor, he had acquired invaluable knowledge of the coastline and potential landing sites.

Hovering helicopters lowered missile launchers for air defence. By dawn, they had established a secure beachhead, taking the Argentine defenders by surprise. The BBC's Robert Fox, going ashore with the troops, described on Friday, 21 May, how they were back on Falklands soil:

The assault force approached the Falklands in ideal conditions. Thick cloud, driving rain and a gale. I embarked with a parachute battalion in four landing craft, exactly the D-Day model. The force approached a sheltered inlet with a hamlet of a few houses and a jetty. Only a few dogs barked. It appeared that surprise was complete. Then the dramatic moment of the ramp going down and the dash up the beach. Now this is the moment we have been waiting for. The ramp is down. We are going forward. I am in the water and I'm on the beach now. We're going ashore with paratroopers heavily laden with missiles and guns. It is a very quiet night, a silent night and now we're ashore. A parachute force is back on the Falklands. During the landings at different points in the creek and anchorage there was persistent naval bombardment. The night air was thick with cordite. Only one of the units, another paratroop battalion, encountered resistance ashore. They had a brisk firefight and there were Argentine casualties and prisoners. They were brought back to the liner *Canberra* which has a comprehensive hospital. Doctors struggled with rudimentary Spanish to reassure the Argentine wounded who appeared to be in their teens mostly. Throughout the night *Canberra* has been the target of continuous attack by aircraft, and the troops digging in on high ground have been watched by the unpleasant Pucara anti-guerrilla aircraft. I saw three of these hugging the contours of the hills as the Paras dug desperately in the peat.

Brian Hanrahan also went ashore at night:

The landing was carried out by stealth rather than force. The ships moved into the main channel between the Falklands and dropped anchor safe from the sight of an Argentine garrison only by the dark moonless night. For the next few hours, the troops clambered down scrambling nets lashed alongside into the landing craft that shuffled back and forth to the shore. It was an agonisingly long operation, nearly four hours from start to finish. All carried out in total silence, both real silence and radio silence. I saw the dark bulk of the landing craft move up alongside the ship, guided only by the short stabs of the luminous wand on the deck. It showed only the merest glimpse of navigation lights to mark its place and the stars just caught the flash of the

White Ensign fluttering at the stern before it was swallowed up by the darkness. Several ships started to bombard the shoreline, not intensively but making it look like a repeat of the shelling which has been happening nightly at points round the Island.

Two graphic eyewitness accounts that described history as it happened.

19

WARSHIPS BLASTED IN 'BOMB ALLEY'

Air raids' heavy toll. Hanrahan on Harriers: 'I counted them all out and I counted them all back.' BBC accused in bombs row.

The lull did not last long before the fury of Argentine air force retaliation, described by Brian Hanrahan on Saturday, 22 May:

It was a brilliantly clear dawn, a beautiful day, a clear one, clear enough to see the troops climbing up the hillside as they secured the bridgehead, clear enough to see the first settlement to fall back under British control, thirty-one people, six children back under the British umbrella, their white cottages tucked into the rolling pastures where the sheep were grazing. But it was clear too for the enemy aircraft that came to find the fleet and attack. The air attack started an hour after dawn and continued right through the day. First came the small Pucara bombers' ground attack, low and surprising. One of them got right into the bay to drop its bombs but without success. For a few moments the air was full of missiles as the defending ships fired back. I saw one Pucara making off over a hill with a missile chasing it. The captain saw a flash in the sky and debris tumbling down. That set the pattern for the rest of the day. Wave after wave of air attacks came against the fleet. First, they had to fight or outwit the Harriers which were between them and the Islands. Then they had to go through the task force frigates and destroyers which were deployed to put up a missile stream but still some of the attacking planes got through to where we were anchored. This morning two Mirages came sweeping down across the bay. We did not see them at first. We saw the red wake of the anti-aircraft missiles rushing out to meet them. Then there was a roar of their engines, the explosion of bombs, missiles, everybody firing together. One stray missile went off in the air only about 100 yards away. Two bombs exploded harmlessly in the hill tops as the planes curved away, diving back where they came from. As the day went on more of the attacks came from the Skyhawk fighter-bombers. In one short period ten or a dozen dived down on the ships at anchor, producing the same barrage of fire and counter-fire. This time there was a new element. The anti-aircraft batteries on the shore joined in. Slowly a defensive screen was being built over the bay, and the worst period of our vulnerability was over. Throughout the day, beneath the air attacks, the helicopters kept on flying. They stayed below radar range. They left the air above clear for the missiles. But they went on ferrying men and machinery and all the equipment that the troops need to build a secure bridge-head. They also brought in, most urgently of all, the anti-aircraft batteries that are being built on the shores alongside us to secure the beachhead and make it safe for all the troops to move through in their bid to recapture the Falkland Islands.

These intensive raids in what the British called 'Bomb Alley' persisted until the end of the campaign. Argentine pilots launched daring, devastating raids on the British ships. On the first day of combat, fifty-seven sorties were flown and 20 tons of bombs dropped. They suffered heavy losses. Twenty-two aircraft were shot down, and fifty-five Argentine airmen lost their lives. They won praise from the British for their bravery and flying prowess.

Senior commanders like Admirals Lewin and Leach steadied nerves with their experience of much worse ship and aircraft losses in the Second World War. On 21 May, the frigate HMS *Ardent* was sunk, as was HMS *Antelope*, whose death throes on 24 May were graphically described by Brian Hanrahan:

Antelope went the way of the other two ships so far, destroyed in a fire started by enemy action. She was hit when the Argentine air force resumed its raids on San Carlos Bay. Although only a few planes broke through the defensive screen, *Antelope* was badly damaged. She came slowly up the bay making smoke, her main mast bent over at an angle. There were holes all along her side and she dropped anchor half a mile away. About an hour after dark there was an explosion on board. A fire started amidships and spread swiftly from the water line to the deck. Smoke and steam sent a grey cloud drifting over the water and through it the searchlights of helicopters probing for survivors. Landing craft came alongside to lift off the crew and transfer them to other ships nearby. We could just see the figures crossing the deck silhouetted by the flames. Other ships and more helicopters quartered the sea round about in case anyone was in the cold waters. It was a courageous and orderly rescue against the ever present danger of further explosion. After everyone had been got clear there were explosions. They sent sparks and flames high into the air and the ship burned white hot through the night. On the deck near me, as I imagine on others in the anchorage, small knots of men looked on in horror as the ship died. At dawn it was still glowing red, the side ripped open, everything above deck level reduced to mangled black metal. On Monday afternoon

Antelope broke her back and as the sea rushed in a white cloud erupted, the hot metal was finally cooled, the bows and the stern rose from the surface then slowly sank.

The destroyer HMS *Coventry* and Cunard cargo vessel *Atlantic Conveyor* were sunk on 25 May. Astonishingly, as one of the cargo ship's engineer officers, Charles Drought, told me, *Atlantic Conveyor* had sailed without chaff defence against missile attack as an 'economy' measure. It was an expensive 'economy' that cost the task force dear. The trajectory of the Exocets had been diverted from their original targets by chaff defence and locked on to the transport ship carrying vital cargo of runway-building equipment, tents, and troop carrier Chinook helicopters. One Chinook had taken off earlier. The helicopter losses slowed down and made much more strenuous the ground force advance and so prolonged the war.

Among the warship decoys to draw away Argentine aircraft from other ships in San Carlos Bay, HMS *Argonaut* and HMS *Brilliant*, both frigates, were badly damaged. The toll might well have been much worse if the Argentine pilots, attempting to avoid anti-aircraft fire and Harrier attack, had not at first dropped bombs from very low altitude. As a consequence, the bomb fuses did not have time to arm before impact. These bombs, some of them sold to the Argentines by Britain, were slowed in descent by a parachute allowing the attacking aircraft to escape damage from the explosion. Thirteen bombs hit British ships without detonating. Lord David Craig, a retired Marshal of the Royal Air Force, remarked: 'A few better fuses and we would have lost the war.'

A BBC broadcast based on a Ministry of Defence briefing in London revealed that the bombs were failing to explode. The pilots changed tactics to make sure the bombs did go off. As the warships faced the fury of air attacks, British warplanes were hitting back, pounding Argentine forces on land. Brian Hanrahan coined one of the most memorable quotes of the war in a despatch describing a British raid without loss:

At dawn our Sea Harriers took off, each carrying three 1,000lb bombs. They wheeled in the skies before heading for the Islands just 90 miles away. Some of the planes went to create more havoc at Stanley and others to a small air strip at Goose Green near Darwin 120 miles to the west. There they found and bombed a number of grounded aircraft mixed in with decoys. At Stanley the planes went in low in waves just seconds apart. They glimpsed the bomb craters left by the Vulcans and left behind them more fire and destruction. The pilots said there had been smoke and dust everywhere punctuated by the flash of explosions. They faced a barrage of return fire, heavy but apparently ineffective. I am not allowed to say how many planes joined the raid. But I counted them all out and I counted them all back. Their pilots were unhurt, cheerful and jubilant. Giving thumbs up signs. One plane had a single bullet hole through the tail. It has already been repaired.

20

BATTLE OF GOOSE GREEN, DEATH OF A HERO

Colonel killed leading assault. Paratroopers win pivotal battle.

The wider scenario did not augur well for the land battles ahead – so many ships lost (four sunk within five days of the British landings and five damaged), the devastating Argentine air attacks, three of the four British troop-carrying Chinook helicopters lost, bad weather, and Argentine troops outnumbering the British by a daunting ratio, fighting from well prepared, sheltered positions.

With his beachhead established, Brigadier Thompson would have preferred to by-pass the Argentine garrison at the twin settlements of Darwin and Goose Green for a 50-mile advance to capture the hill positions around Stanley. But he received a direct order from London to attack the settlements. He was under pressure from the UK politicians, who wanted quick action to maintain the momentum of the campaign and to placate worried public opinion at home, and also from the Royal Navy under unsustainable air attacks and threatened by approaching Antarctic winter gales forcing the fleet to withdraw.

The task was given to the second battalion of the Parachute Regiment, 2 Para, whose regimental motto 'Ready for Anything' did not prepare them for the conditions they encountered in this battle, testing their endurance and resolve to the limit. But they

lived up to the nickname given them by their German oppo-
nents in the Second World War – 'the Red Devils', reflecting
their fearsome reputation and the colour of their berets.

The commanding officer, Lieutenant Colonel H. Jones, having
seen intelligence reports revealing Argentine troop positions
and capability, realised his troops were sharing the same hill as
the enemy.

The situation could hardly get worse. But it did, no thanks
to the BBC in a serious breach of security. The World Service
broadcast that British troops were poised to advance on Goose
Green. Lieutenant Colonel H. Jones was furious and ordered
his troops to disperse in anticipation of an air strike. It did not
materialise. But the Argentines, now on alert, flew in reinforcements by helicopter.

On the night of 27/28 May, only a week after landing at San
Carlos and walking, heavily laden, into position, about 600 men
of 2 Para, with only light artillery and engineer support, attacked
the 12th Infantry Regiment defending Darwin and Goose
Green commanded by Lieutenant Colonel Ítalo Ángel Piaggi.

The advance began in darkness at 2.30 a.m. over difficult terrain in biting wind and bitter cold, turning to heavy rain. The
British were outnumbered by a stubborn enemy, entrenched in
positions overlooking open ground sloping upwards, enabling
them to concentrate rifle, machine gun, mortar and more powerful longer-range artillery. The battalion was left to fight only
with rifle, grenade, machine gun, light anti-tank guns and only
two mortars, which fired more than 1,000 bombs, the vibration
causing them to sink into the soft ground.

Carrier-launched Harriers had attacked the settlements briefly
in preceding days, but the paratroopers had no air support for the
initial stages of the battle, and an inshore bombardment by the

frigate HMS *Arrow* was interrupted for two hours by a technical malfunction in the frigate's gun turret. It was resumed at 4.30 a.m. for fifty minutes when the frigate should have retreated earlier in darkness to the safety of air cover at San Carlos.

It took fourteen hours of close-quarter fighting to move 6 kilometres. With his troops pinned down by incessant firing, the battle stalled.

'Colonel H', as he was known, sensed that a critical, decisive moment had been reached. Leading from the front, he set off on his doomed charge towards the enemy machine gun trenches, firing his sub-machine gun. He was hit and rolled backwards but rose to his feet and charged forward, only to be shot a second time. He died on the battlefield. The dramatic message was relayed back to headquarters: 'Sunray is down.'

Five officers and men who charged forward with him were also killed. The Argentines used commando-trained snipers to deadly effect. One sniper alone killed seven Paras.

Colonel H had been determined to press on with the assault in the belief that, in the words of General Wilsey, 'his men could, would and indeed had to deliver a positive outcome – even without him, a possibility he had always acknowledged'.

The colonel's actions came in for high praise, coupled with criticism, accusing him of reckless impetuosity and foolhardiness. He was defended by his friend, General John Wilsey, in a book entitled *H. Jones VC: the Life and Death of an Unusual Hero*. Wilsey writes:

> Colonel H was stubborn and impatient. But his virtues were noble and strong: courage, honour, loyalty and devotion to true friends and cause alike. His intense commitment and profound sense of duty were likely to demand and secure the ultimate sacrifice. He rose to meet his destiny and his death.

He was awarded the Commonwealth's highest honour for gallantry, the Victoria Cross. His citation said, 'this devastating display of courage had a shattering effect on the enemy and completely undermined their will to fight'. But this assessment is challenged in the official account of the war by Professor Lawrence Freedman. He said it was 'the stuff of legend' but had only a modest impact on the battle and probably affected the Paras more than the enemy.

Robert Fox had become friends with Colonel H and described the sad recovery of his body from the hillside and those of the five soldiers who died with him:

> Quietly two men were sent up to bring down 'H' and Captain David Wood, the adjutant, an extremely popular figure as indeed were all these men, particularly the young corporals … They brought down the colonel on a stretcher. The sun had gone. There was just a faint glow of twilight. It was silhouette. They carried the body down slowly and a soldier walked in front with the three weapons of the three officers sluing over his back and pointing to the ground. It was a silent and just tribute to the heroism of everybody that day.

A helicopter flying in to evacuate the colonel's body as well as the wounded was shot down by a Pucara, and the pilot was killed.

There were many other heroes that day, and many more hours of fighting to come. Success was achieved not by one astounding act of gallantry but by the bravery and fighting qualities of the whole battalion.

In the advance on the airfield, Argentines were seen waving white flags in what seemed to be a local truce. Lieutenant James Barry and Corporal Paul Sullivan moved forward to accept what they assumed was surrender, but the Argentines opened fire without warning. Barry got tangled in barbed wire and was killed, and Sullivan wounded. An Argentine crawled forward to shoot Sullivan in the head at point-blank range.

This prompted Sergeant John Meredith to charge forward with his machine gun, killing four Argentines and saving several British troops. He too was awarded a gallantry medal, which had a surprise sequel. After forty years' service, John Meredith sold this and all his other medals in 2020 for £150,000 to fund his retirement. What price courage?

One of the least experienced Paras, Graham Carter, led the rest of the platoon with fixed bayonets to capture the airfield. He was awarded the Military Medal.

Near the airfield, one unit strayed unknowingly into a minefield in darkness, taking shelter in hollows they thought had been made by exploding shells. Only at dawn as they tiptoed out of the minefield over tripwires did they discover the holes had been caused by wandering cows treading on anti-personnel landmines!

With Colonel H dead, his second-in-command, Major Chris Keeble, took charge with determination, courage, and cool, calculated reassessment. Keeble faced almost insuperable challenges, worsened by lack of resupply, not just of ammunition but food rations and replacement clothing, right down to warm, dry socks.

As the British advanced across open, treeless, rocky terrain, they came under attack from fearsome Pucara aircraft armed with bombs, machine guns and napalm, which drenched some Paras but did not ignite. Argentine aircraft controlled the skies. Due to thick sea mist, the Harriers tasked with attacking Argentine positions were prevented from taking off from the carriers for hours.

Brigadier Thompson told Keeble he could destroy Goose Green settlement, if necessary, to force surrender. But this could not be contemplated when he discovered from Islanders freed from Darwin that there were 114 civilians incarcerated in Goose Green Community Hall, including the elderly and more than forty children and babies.

Under fire from machine guns and pounded by artillery out of range of the British guns, there seemed no end to this battle.

To Keeble, the situation looked precarious. His companies were exhausted, cold, and running out of water, food and ammunition. More Argentine reinforcements, dropped by helicopter, could counterattack. Delayed Harrier strikes, guided in with skill to avoid the nearby British advance patrols, missed their targets.

Keeble, fatigued from non-stop fighting against near-impossible odds, said to himself: 'How the hell do I capture Goose Green?' He was to answer his own question later with a surrender ultimatum.

Keeble was a tough paratroop officer but also a compassionate, committed Christian – a Roman Catholic, as were most Argentines. These qualities influenced his thinking, prompting him to draft a surrender ultimatum. His persuasive document in Spanish is worth quoting in full:

To the Commander, Argentine armed forces, Darwin/Goose Green area.

Military Options:

We have sent a prisoner of war under a white flag to convey the following military options:

That you surrender your force to us by leaving the township, forming up in a military manner, removing your helmets and laying down your weapons. You will give prior notice of this intention by returning the POW under the white flag with him briefed as to formalities no later than 0830 local time.

You refuse in the first case to surrender and take the inevitable consequence. You will give prior notice of this intention by returning the POW without his white flag (though his neutrality will be respected) no later than 0830 hours local.

In any event and in accordance with the terms of the Geneva Conventions and Laws of War you shall be held responsible for the fate of any civilians in Darwin or Goose Green and we in accordance with those laws do give you prior notice of our intention to bombard Darwin/Goose Green.

Signed: C. Keeble, Commander British Forces, Darwin/Goose Green area.

The Argentine commanders learned of the ultimatum from the civilian managers at Goose Green and Port San Carlos on the Island civilian radio net. Major Keeble and his fellow officers walked to the airfield, where two hours of discussion led to a 'dignified surrender' on what was Argentine National Army Day (29 May). When Air Commodore Wilson Doser Pedroza agreed the surrender terms, Major Keeble said he would like to visit Argentina. Air Commodore Pedroza remarked: 'You are already in Argentina!' Defiant even in defeat.

A signal was flashed to London: 'The Union Jack has just been raised over Goose Green settlement.' That night, snow began to fall.

Keeble's persuasive words had proved more powerful than weapons in shortening the battle and saving the lives of troops and civilians alike.

The British lost eighteen killed (sixteen Paras, one Royal Marine pilot, and one commando sapper) and sixty-four wounded.

The Argentines lost forty-five men killed and ninety wounded, and 1,100 taken prisoner. Classic military doctrine stipulates that attackers should outnumber defenders by at least two-to-one. This battle was the other way round – nearly two-to-one in favour of the Argentine defenders.

Brigadier Thompson paid tribute to 'the magnificent fighting spirit of the Parachute Battalion under the leadership of Lieutenant Colonel H. Jones'. Congratulating Keeble, Admiral Fieldhouse declared: 'You have kindled a flame in land operations.'

The Argentine commander, Lieutenant Colonel Piaggi, was forced to resign from the army and faced several trials questioning his competence. In his defence, he cited lack of logistical support from the generals in Stanley as he had no mortar rounds left and few artillery shells. It took ten years before Piaggi had his military rank and pay reinstated. He died in 2012.

Keeble's leadership was a key factor in securing capitulation. He was more flexible than Jones, giving his company commanders more autonomy. He was awarded a DSO (Distinguished Service Order). His achievement was overshadowed by the heroism of Colonel H but should not be underestimated. His soldiers wanted him to continue as their commander, but he was replaced by Lieutenant Colonel David Chaundler, from the UK, who dropped by parachute to take over.

Robert Fox, in his book acknowledging the paratroopers' fearsome fighting reputation, said he found other qualities among 'the most civilised men he had ever been in a tight corner with'. 'Their standard of personal generosity, of kindness, of respect for human life is of a very high degree indeed, and that says a lot for their efficiency. They are such good fighting troops because they care about each other desperately as individuals.'

21

GOOSE GREEN: CRUCIAL TURNING POINT

Victory prevents humiliating task force withdrawal and total defeat. Reinforcements give impetus to advance.

Early in the campaign, Admiral John Woodward had said his biggest enemy was time:

> Failure by the land force commander to win the land battle by mid to late June will cause him to lose it because the Navy Battle Group will lose it for him. We will simply be unable to support and protect him. We will be unable to go on fighting. There will be nothing left out here to fight with.

Admiral Sir John Fieldhouse warned the army that rather than lose more ships, he was ready to lift the troops off the beaches unless progress was made. Failure to seize Darwin and Goose Green in the first land battle of the campaign would have resulted in humiliating British defeat and abandonment of the Islands, leaving the Argentines triumphantly in control and the Islanders trapped under brutal military rule.

The Chief of the General Staff and head of the army, Field Marshal Lord Bramall, a veteran of the Second World War, told me: 'If Goose Green had been lost, the whole campaign would have been lost.'

Paratroop Colonel (later General) Hew Pike said the victory over a much larger force gave the British 'moral ascendancy' and the knowledge that 'we could win'.

Margaret Thatcher said Colonel H. Jones's sacrifice, matchless heroism and leadership demonstrated British resolve to reclaim the Islands.

The civilians were liberated unharmed. A woman Islander said, 'We were so relieved. I cried.' The Islanders gave their liberators a memorable welcome as Robert Fox captured the moment:

After a whole day's bitter fighting and morning of delicate surrender negotiations, the cheer of liberation came in the early afternoon. Women handed round cups of tea in Royal wedding mugs. Children carried round tins of cakes and biscuits to the young Paras, their faces still camouflaged and their eyes bleary with exhaustion. For nearly a month the 114 people had been shut in the community hall by the Argentines. Their houses had been raided, with their furniture smashed and excrement on the floor. The store had been looted. The Argentine soldiers were underfed, and in one house used by pilots it seemed that the officers had been hoarding tinned food. The Argentines committed acts of petty meanness, smashing and stealing radios and shooting at a shepherd from a helicopter as he tended his sheep.

Hampered by the loss of the troop-carrying helicopters sunk on *Atlantic Conveyor* only three days before the battle of Goose Green, men of 45 Commando and of the Parachute Regiment began an exhausting 50-mile march across East Falkland towards their main objective, Port Stanley. With one battle won, there were another eight to fight, all mountain strongholds with Argentine forces entrenched on the summits behind natural boulder barricades.

Between battles, the British forces 'yomped' on foot over rocks and through boggy peat, their boots sinking at every step, and so heavily burdened with equipment, equal to their own body weight, that when they fell down, frequently, they could not get up without being lifted by colleagues. Their uniforms were wet through with nowhere and no way to dry them. They had few tents for cover. Lying down, the soldiers erected personal shelters from their poncho capes reinforced with wood and rocks, as they lay in shallow hollows which filled with water from the boggy ground.

The Royal Marines and the Parachute Regiment, along with elite units of the SAS (Special Air Service) and the SBS (Special Boat Service), are the fittest, best trained of British Forces. They needed to be.

During Harrier missions on 30 May, Squadron Leader Jerry Pook was shot down by small-arms fire, the only RAF pilot to die. He was awarded the Distinguished Flying Cross.

Another pilot, Jeff Glover, was injured when he ejected from his Harrier, hit by a missile. He landed by parachute in the water and was rescued and given medical aid by the Argentines.

On 31 May, Mount Kent and Mount Challenger were captured, and on 3 June, the British occupied the settlements at Fitzroy and Bluff Cove, to advance on Stanley from the south. But troops transported there by ship were attacked before getting ashore.

22

TROOPSHIPS BOMBED, MANY CASUALTIES

Troops trapped in blazing landing craft. Gallant helicopter rescues as *Sir Galahad* burns.

Deadly dawn air assaults caught troop-laden landing craft *Sir Galahad* and *Sir Tristram* unawares anchored in Port Pleasant, near Fitzroy. They were sitting targets for a devastating bombing raid on 8 June, which set the ships ablaze, trapping many troops below decks to die in agony. The attack was described by Brian Hanrahan:

> The landing ships were unloading men and materials when a formation of Skyhawks came in low from the direction of the sea. Both ships were hit and sustained damage. From just over a ridge I watched a column of grey smoke slowly turn to black as fire aboard *Sir Galahad* spread swiftly. The sea around the ship blossomed in orange dots as men jumped over the side into life rafts. The helicopters which had been moving stores clustered about her pulling men from the decks and the water. From the flames came a steady rattle of exploding ammunition. Ignoring the background clatter and an occasional bigger explosion, the rescuing helicopters plunged into the smoke risking their own lives to save others. One helicopter was completely masked by the black cloud as it tried repeatedly to winch a man from the water close

by the side of the ship. Fortunately, the cliffs were close by and the helicopters dropped the survivors there and turned back to resume their search for more survivors. They clustered around the front of the ship all but masking it from view. Then they started to search the water out over the bay for anybody who had been missed. By this time medical teams had been set up on the cliffs to treat the casualties before Land Rovers took their charges away to the field hospital. In the midst of all this there was another air raid but the medics worked on unmindful of the boxes of ammunition stacked nearby. One of the sergeants had to order them to split up in case there was a hit near them. Other survivors came off unhurt but badly shaken. They wandered dazed among the muddy paths still wearing their life jackets and orange survival suits those who'd had time to put them on. Some of the soldiers still had camouflage cream smeared on their faces. They said the ship had filled with smoke almost immediately it was hit.

Survivors began arriving on board *Fearless*, Welsh Guardsmen, bewildered and shocked after their first taste of action. All had blackened faces. Many bore the gruesome evidence of flash burns. It had been a feature of this raid that so suddenly had the fighters arrived, no one had time to pull on their protective face masks and gloves. One bomb came right through the hatch to the tank deck where the men were gathering prior to disembarking for Fitzroy settlement. Blown across the deck, many found themselves shrouded in smoke and desperately searching for a way out. Casualties were taken to safety in minutes. Helicopters are on the scene within minutes. Both *Sir Galahad* and *Sir Tristram* were abandoned. It had been the heaviest and costliest air attack that week. It was a gruesome reminder that the Argentine air force was still a potent weapon. Several of the attacking aircraft were shot down by Harriers.

The raid caused the highest British casualties in any single attack: forty-eight dead, thirty-two of them Welsh Guardsmen, and 115 wounded. They included Simon Weston, whose badly scarred face became a badge of courage, masking the hidden anguish of mental stress. He described to me the trauma of being trapped in a blazing ship and suffering numerous operations and years of pain in his remarkable recovery from horrific burns. Some soldiers had miraculous escapes. One medic, Clive Tilsley, told me how he was trapped with others below decks in the bowels of the burning ship. Through the smoke, they spotted high above them a patch of bright sky. They helped each other scramble up the decks, haul themselves through the hole onto the hot deck, and throw themselves into the sea. Their escape hole had been made by an Argentine bomb.

Confusion and changes of plan had delayed a swift landing, ignoring Major Southby-Tailyour's orders to disembark immediately. A day of disaster was also a day of immense courage as navy helicopters hovered above the stricken ships to winch survivors to safety. The helicopter crews won praise for their bravery and determination in countless rescues. One of the pilots was the Queen's son, Prince Andrew, who was the focus for Argentine sarcasm. Rejecting a call by Admiral Woodward to surrender after the first British air raids, General Menéndez replied: 'No way. We are winning. Bring your little Prince and come and get us.'

23

MOUNTAIN STRONGHOLDS FALL, SUDDEN SURRENDER

Another Victoria Cross hero. A welcome cup of tea for the General.

The attack on the landing ships failed to stall the British offensive. On 11 June, supported by naval gunfire, a night attack against the heavily defended high ground around Stanley captured Mount Harriet, Two Sisters, and Mount Longdon, where Falkland Islanders fought alongside the paratroopers and drove ammunition supplies up the mountain and ferried back the wounded. It was here that Sergeant Ian McKay of the 3rd Battalion of the Parachute Regiment was killed charging and destroying an Argentine position holding up the attack. He was awarded the second Victoria Cross of the campaign for what his citation called 'outstanding selflessness, perseverance and courage … With complete disregard for his own safety … And leadership of the highest order.'

With tank support, 2nd Battalion of the Parachute Regiment captured Wireless Ridge and Two Sisters Mountain. The 2nd Battalion of the Scots Guards, with Royal Marines and Gurkhas, supported by naval frigate bombardment, took Mount Tumbledown in a final ferocious battle. This lasted twelve hours, mostly fought at night against stubborn defenders who repeatedly counterattacked. Close-quarter fighting involved bayonet attacks led by Major (later General) John Kiszely, who was awarded the Military Cross.

As the last mountain strongholds fell, Stanley was within reach. Both sides were running short of ammunition. Argentine morale was ebbing away as they were pounded by artillery and naval gunfire, and casualties mounted.

For General Menéndez and General Oscar Jofre, tasked with the defence of Stanley, the military position was untenable. The humanitarian consequences of continuing were horrendous, a bloodbath of mass casualties among military combatants and civilians. There were danger signs that the Stanley garrison, facing defeat, might vent their anger on civilians. Soldiers deliberately set civilian houses on fire.

As detailed in his book, an Argentine conscript told Max Hastings, one of the first correspondents to enter Stanley with the advancing troops: 'No one really knew what the orders were, whether we should go on fighting or not. We were all very nervous. Our platoon commander, Lieutenant Freeba, told us to take positions in the houses. "If a Kelper resists, shoot him."'

General Jofre, whom I interviewed after the war, was worried that many of his soldiers were in a strange state of mind and that many civilians would get hurt. Jofre told me he was worried that he was no longer in control and that discipline would break down. He and General Menéndez realised it was no use continuing to resist. They agreed it was 'all over' and they should arrange a ceasefire.

Others disagreed. A major planted booby traps around Government House and set fire to premises used as ammunition dumps. He fired his rifle at British troops in the hope of provoking them to break a ceasefire.

British forces had superiority at sea, on land, and in the air. Argentine troops were retreating. In a radio conversation with

Galteiri, Menéndez said his forces could not continue fighting. Sacrificing soldiers' lives in a hopeless situation was worse than surrender. Galtieri said his intelligence staff told him the British were in a similarly precarious position. He angrily told Menéndez to counterattack in a last-ditch defence of Stanley to salvage national pride. Menéndez told him the Argentine position was unsustainable.

Menéndez said there had been no intention to fight in the town. A good general must know when a battle is lost. Without victory, it was no use losing lives just for the sake of it. Argentines believed the Malvinas were Argentine. But they did not hate the Islanders.

In fact, no civilians were shot. General Menéndez, whom I later interviewed in Buenos Aires, said he wanted to avoid a humanitarian disaster. He received repeated British requests to 'surrender with honour'. They emphasised Britain's humanitarian interest in avoiding civilian casualties and the destruction of the Argentine forces.

On 9 June, negotiations for a ceasefire began when Doctor Alison Bleaney, who had maintained a radio medical service to isolated settlements, heard a message from Royal Marines Captain Rod Bell, who spoke Spanish and had helped to achieve the ceasefire at Goose Green.

SAS Colonel (later General) Michael Rose was tasked to contact the Argentine commanders to seek surrender of their 11,000 troops. Rose shouted over the radio: 'Fetch officer. I am British High Command.' Back came a reply, in impeccable English, from Captain Barry Hussey, which began five days of negotiations. Rose's messages, stressing the futile predicament of the Argentine forces, were reinforced between 11–13 June by British seizure of the cragged peaks commanding the approach to Stanley. The Argentines had regiments of artillery and lots of food, but British forces were down to the bare minimum. The fleet had only seven days of supplies left.

Rose was experienced in psychological persuasion, which he had used during the SAS siege and capture of the Iranian embassy in London two years earlier. This time the hostages were hundreds of civilians in Stanley. Rose told Hussey that the fighting had to stop.

On 14 June, Menéndez allowed Rose and Bell to fly into Stanley by helicopter trailing a white flag. Rose insisted on the surrender of all Argentine forces, not just on East Falkland as Menéndez offered. Rose told him the surrender should be 'honourable', not humiliating, and should exclude the word 'unconditional'. Six hours of heated negotiations were at an end.

In a heavy snowstorm, Major General Moore flew in to accept the surrender, still in battle dress grimy from his muddy mountaintop headquarters. He was met by an immaculately uniformed General Menéndez. General Moore signalled the surrender to London: 'The Falkland Islands are once again living under the Government of their choice.'

He described the historic moment in an on-the-spot interview with Brian Hanrahan:

General Menéndez has surrendered forces on the Falkland Islands, both East and West, 11,000 of them, a lot to be sorted out. The Argentines have fought very bravely. I am not surprised at the outcome because of the superb quality of the men I have been commanding whose training is excellent, whose determination, drive and energy in very, very difficult conditions in the mountains, hard weather, hard country and a determined enemy, have made it a jolly hard slog. They have marched from the far end of this island to this end of it and they are fit and ready to go as ever.

The logistic achievement on top of the achievement of sheer fighting and guts is absolutely colossal. The way the navy have kept the supplies coming despite their losses has been a very brave effort. Logistic work has been done to get stuff forward over this very difficult country where there are no roads and no lorries to carry it. It had to be got from ship to shore round the coast into the little harbours and taken forward by helicopters. It has been a tremendous effort. Helicopter pilots have been flying very bravely to get casualties out, all day and half the night. It has been a damn close-run thing. Some of my guns this morning with 400 rounds a gun were down to twenty.

The surrender prompted Thatcher's famous 'Rejoice! Rejoice!' rejoinder to journalists outside 10 Downing Street. Galtieri learned of the surrender as he attended a Mass conducted by the Pope visiting Buenos Aires.

Brigadier Thompson, whose inspirational leadership contributed so much to victory, learned of the surrender from a BBC World Service broadcast. 'We heard the terms of the surrender from a news flash broadcast from London 8,000 miles away describing events that had just taken place 800 metres down the road from where we sat. It was an emotional moment.'

In victory, radio was first with news of the surrender, as it had been with news of the invasion. Radio had an instantaneous impact in this war, sometimes positive and sometimes negative, but always the great communicator. Even Thatcher said she was 'glued' to the radio.

General Moore was cheered and lifted shoulder-high by grateful Islanders when he walked into the West Store supermarket, one of the buildings marked out as a safe shelter for civilians. General Moore turned to broadcaster Patrick Watts and said: 'I could do with a good cup of tea.' Patrick told me he said: 'Come to my place.' And there, in Patrick's lounge, the General enjoyed the best cup of tea of his life, very well-earned.

At Government House, Rose took down from the wall a picture of Galtieri and replaced it with a portrait of the Queen he found in a broom cupboard. The Argentine generals occupying Government House had never destroyed it, their senior intelligence officer told me, 'out of respect for the Queen'!

Rose acquired for his regiment a unique souvenir: an equestrian statue of General José de San Martín, hero of Argentina's struggle for independence from Spain. It had been presented to Menéndez by Galtieri to commemorate the 'liberation of the Malvinas'. The statue's new location was the SAS officers' mess at Hereford.

Don Bonner, Rex Hunt's chauffeur, had persuaded the Argentines to let him check on Government House and its furniture throughout the occupation to discourage any damage. He told Argentine troops not to station guns around Government House so as to avoid drawing artillery fire into the civilian community.

Thousands of Argentine troops abandoned their positions and streamed into Stanley. Amid this mayhem, one of my Falklands friends, Cecil Bertrand, a veteran of the Antarctic whaling era, now in his seventies, went out to plant his potatoes. I asked him why. He replied in a literally down-to-earth way: 'If I did not plant my potatoes, I would not get a crop next season.' This typical stoicism and pragmatic self-reliance demonstrated to me why the Islanders will never surrender their independence to Argentine blandishments.

Repatriation of prisoners to Argentina began at once, more than 4,000 crammed, ironically, on the *Canberra*, which had brought British troops south. A plot by other Argentine prisoners to hijack the merchant vessel *NoTland* taking them to Argentina was thwarted when their coded messages between cabins were detected by a Spanish-speaking British soldier.

A plan by Admiral Anaya called 'Operation Algeciras', to send a guerrilla group of underwater swimmers to sink British ships in Gibraltar, failed when the saboteurs, targeting the BP *British Tamar*, were arrested by Spanish police. Their movements had been monitored by the intelligence services in France and Spain.

On 20 June, the Argentines on Southern Thule, undisturbed for six years since 1976, surrendered on board *Endurance*, whose commander, Nick Barker, had first detected the garrison. Hostilities were at an end.

Bravest of the Brave

The many medals awarded included the Victoria Cross, the Commonwealth's highest award for gallantry, for two men, killed in two crucial battles, one at the start and the other near the end of the land campaign. Their citations deserve to be recorded in full:

Lt. Colonel Herbert Jones OBE, The Parachute Regiment

On 28 May 1982 Lieutenant Colonel Jones was commanding 2nd battalion The Parachute Regiment on operations on the Falkland Islands. The Battalion was ordered to attack enemy positions in and around the settlements of Darwin and Goose Green. During the attack against an enemy, who was well dug in with mutually supporting positions sited in depth, the battalion was held up just South of Darwin by a particularly well-prepared and resilient enemy position of at least 11 trenches on an important ridge.

A number of casualties were received. In order to read the battle fully and ensure that the momentum of his attack was not lost, Colonel Jones took forward his reconnaissance party to the foot of a re-entrant which a section of his battalion had just secured. Despite persistent, heavy and accurate fire the reconnaissance party gained the top of the re-entrant, at approximately the same time as the enemy positions.

In his effort to gain a good viewpoint, Colonel Jones was now at the very front of his battalion. It was clear to him that desperate measures were needed in order to overcome the enemy position and rekindle the attack, and that unless these measures were taken promptly the battalion would sustain increasing casualties and the attack perhaps even fail. It was time for personal leadership and action. Colonel Jones immediately seized a sub-machine gun, and, calling on those around him and with total disregard for his own safety, charged the nearest enemy position. This action exposed him to fire from a number of trenches.

As he charged up a short slope at the enemy position he was seen to fall and roll backward downhill. He immediately picked himself up, and charged the enemy trench firing his sub-machine gun and seemingly oblivious to the intense fire directed at him. He was hit by fire from another trench which he outflanked and fell dying only a few feet from the enemy he had assaulted. A short time later a company of the battalion attacked the enemy, who quickly surrendered. The devastating display of courage by Colonel Jones had completely under-mined their will to fight further.

Thereafter the momentum of the attack was rapidly regained, Darwin and Goose Green were liberated, and the battalion released the local inhabitants unharmed and forced the surrender of some 1,200 of the enemy.

The achievements of 2nd Battalion the Parachute Regiment at Darwin and Goose Green set the tone for the subsequent land victory on the Falklands. They achieved such a moral superiority over the enemy in this first battle, that despite the advantages of numbers and selection of battle-ground, they never thereafter doubted either the superior fighting qualities of the British troops, or their own inevitable defeat. This was an action of the utmost gallantry by a commanding officer whose dashing leadership and courage throughout the battle were an inspiration to all about him.

Sergeant Ian John McKay, The Parachute Regiment

During the night of 11/12 June 1982, 3rd Battalion the Parachute regiment mounted a silent night attack on an enemy battalion position on Mount Longdon, an important objective in the battle for Port Stanley in the Falkland Islands. Sergeant McKay was platoon sergeant of 4 Platoon, B Company, which after the initial objective had been secured, was ordered to clear the northern side of the long east/west ridge feature, held by the enemy in depth, with strong mutually supporting positions.

By now the enemy were fully alert and resisting fiercely. As 4 Platoon's advance continued it came under increasingly heavy fire from a number of well-sited enemy machine gun positions on the ridge, and received casualties. Realising that no further advance was possible, the platoon commander ordered the platoon to move from its exposed position to seek shelter among the rocks of the ridge itself. Here it met up with part of 5 Platoon.

The enemy fire was still heavy and accurate, and the position of the platoons was becoming increasingly hazardous. Taking Sergeant McKay, a corporal and a few others, and covered by supporting machine gun fire, the platoon commander moved forward to reconnoitre the enemy positions but was hit by a bullet in the leg, and command devolved upon Sergeant McKay.

It was clear that instant action was needed if the advance was not to falter and increasing casualties to ensue. Sergeant McKay decided to convert this reconnaissance into an attack in order to eliminate the enemy positions. He was in no doubt of the strength and deployment of the enemy as he undertook this attack. He issued orders, and taking three men with him, broke cover and charged the enemy position.

The assault was met by a hail of fire. The corporal was seriously wounded, a private killed and another wounded. Despite these losses, Sergeant McKay, with complete disregard for his own safety, continued to charge the enemy position alone. On reaching it he dispatched the enemy with grenades, thereby relieving the position of beleaguered 4 and 5 Platoons, who were now able to redeploy with relative safety. Sergeant McKay, however, was killed at the moment of victory, his body falling on the bunker.

Without doubt Sergeant McKay's action retrieved a most dangerous situation and was instrumental in ensuring the success of the attack. His was a coolly calculated act, the dangers of which must have been only too apparent to him beforehand. Undeterred he performed with outstanding selflessness, perseverance and courage. With a complete disregard for his own safety, he displayed courage and leadership of the highest order, and was an inspiration to all those around him.

BRAVEST OF THE BRAVE

The two Falklands recipients of the Victoria Cross.

Sergeant Ian McKay VC, killed charging
enemy positions on Mount Longdon.
(Airborne Assault Archives)

Colonel H. Jones VC, shot dead leading
his troops at Darwin – Goose Green.
(Airborne Assault Archives)

Major Chris Keeble, who assumed command and won the battle for Goose Green. (Airborne Assault Archives)

All three were members of the Parachute Regiment which, along with the Royal Marines, bore the brunt of most of the land battles in the advance on Port Stanley.

THE MODERN FALKLANDS

Unprecedented prosperity has brought full employment, low taxes, fully state-funded education, and new infrastructure, thanks to a flourishing new fishery industry, growing wildlife tourism, traditional sheep farming, and offshore oil discoveries.

FV Falcon, a modern squid jigger, joins the fleet. (Fortuna)

Children live naturally with prolific wildlife, which attracts thousands of tourists, many from cruise ship visits. (Derek Pettersson)

Wildlife tourism; penguins are a big attraction for visitors from cruise ships.
(Derek Pettersson)

Multitasking Islander Louise Pole-Evans: sheep farmer, shearer and tourist guide.
(Louise Pole-Evans)

Penguins at Saunders Island.

Offshore oil discoveries could boost future prosperity.

UK LEADERS AND COMMANDERS

British fighting men's capability was complemented by outstanding leaders with vast experience in warfare, including the Second World War. Key figures follow.

Prime Minister Margaret Thatcher talks to the author, Harold Briley, watched by a former Falklands Governor, David Tatham.

Governor and Lady Hunt.
(Courtesy Lady Hunt: Crown Copyright)

Admiral Lord West, whose ship was sunk, became head of the Royal Navy and a Government Security Minister.

Air Chief Marshal Squire, a Harrier pilot, became head of the Royal Air Force.

Brigadier Julian Thompson, whose Royal Marines and Paratroop Brigade won most of the land battles.

Commodore Michael Clapp, who commanded amphibious operations.

Surgeon Commander Rick Jolly saved every injured man, British and Argentine, in his field hospital.

Simon Weston: the face of courage, severely burned in Argentine air raid.

Architect of victory, Admiral Sir Henry Leach, head of the Navy, had his ships ready to sail.

ARGENTINE COMMANDERS

The Argentine commanders had no experience of warfare.

Clockwise from top left: Three-man invasion junta – General Galtieri, Admiral Anaya, Air Force Brigadier Lami Dozo. They were in charge for only the last six months of the six-year dictatorship. Defeat forced their downfall, leading to charges of mismanaging the war, and then to jail for human rights crimes against their own population; President Galtieri; 'Military Governor General Mario Menéndez surrendered to save lives in defiance of General Galtieri's orders to fight on'; Civilian Foreign Minister Costa Mendez, who admitted, 'War was a mistake.' (Martin Arias Feijoo)

The now peaceful Stanley waterfront. The capital has expanded with new roads, new houses, and a new port.

Lord Shackleton greeted by Islanders demanding to remain British. His reports recommended radical reforms for recovery and development which led to huge prosperity.

It took nearly forty years to remove 26,000 Argentine landmines. An Islander remarked: 'We've got our land and beaches back and our freedom to roam.'

Falklands War Memorial in Stanley.

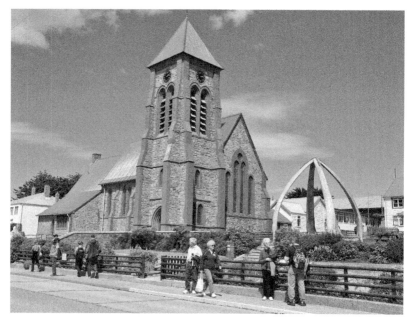

Thanksgiving and memorial services are held in the most southerly Anglican cathedral in the world, with its landmark whalebone arch.

24

THE RED AND GREEN LIFE MACHINE

Medical miracles in disused meat shed amid unexploded bombs. Every wounded man, British or Argentine, was kept alive.

Many of the seriously wounded were brought back from the brink of death by skilful surgery. Not one wounded man taken to the makeshift front-line British field hospital at Ajax Bay near San Carlos for emergency treatment left in a body bag. All were kept alive; 800 British and 200 Argentine, friend and foe, were treated in true compassionate medical tradition.

The outstanding Royal Marines surgeon in charge, Commander Rick Jolly, said in his book:'Everyone who reached Ajax Bay alive has gone out alive. After 107 operations and despite the severe wounding power of modern munitions, it is no mean achievement.' Others would call it miraculous. British doctors worked not in clinically clean hospital conditions but in a disused meat-processing refrigeration plant abandoned thirty years previously. Life-saving operations were performed by the tri-service medical teams during air raids with bombs cascading down. Several bombs exploded among ammunition stored nearby.

In a low-level raid at dusk on 27 May, a bomb exploded in the kitchen, causing more casualties and a fierce fire just as two Argentines were being operated upon. The medical teams threw themselves to the floor, but one steel-helmeted surgeon, Bill McGregor, remained on his feet, covering a stomach wound with gauze.

One unexploded bomb lodged in a wall and another above their heads in the ceiling, which had partly caved in and had to be shored up. A sandbag cordon was built around the bombs, some of which had time-delayed fuses which could set them off within the next thirty-three hours. The surgeons shunned evacuation and worked on regardless.

One day alone, nearly fifty operations were performed when eighty casualties were stretchered in. The strain was almost intolerable, as Dr Jolly remembers: 'An overwhelming, aching tiredness consumes me. Everything is an effort. Decisions are difficult. Tempers are frayed.'

Rick Jolly called this remarkable hospital the 'Red and Green Life Machine', reflecting the colour of the medical teams' berets, Paras and Royal Marines. That was the title of his diaries recording the day-to-day life and near-death drama. Jolly's remarkable leadership won him an OBE from the United Kingdom and a matching medal from Argentina. Doctor McGregor was also awarded an OBE. There is no greater reward than saving lives when others are taking them.

Rick Jolly was young for such an onerous challenge – just 36, but commando-trained and the right man in the right place at the right time.

His field hospital was a vital link in the medical chain from hurriedly applied dressings on the battlefield and the forward emergency medical units at Teal Inlet and Fitzroy, to transfer to the 300-bed converted former schools excursion ship *Uganda*. She had been rapidly converted into a floating hospital with added facilities for refuelling at sea and a helicopter landing pad, enabling casualties to be flown directly from the battlefield to a hospital ship for the first time ever in any conflict. Immediate treatment by hundreds of naval doctors and nurses saved many lives. Fears that *Uganda* would be bombed were unfounded, and Argentine pilots scrupulously respected the big red crosses on its funnel and hull. *Canberra* also had a hospital.

Three survey vessels converted to medical transports – *Hydra, Hecla* and *Hecate* – took the wounded to Uruguay for return by RAF aircraft to Britain. It was testimony to the skill of hundreds of medical staff that only three wounded men died in that long evacuation process. The Argentines treated their wounded at a military hospital in Stanley and in two hospital ships.

Many of the wounded had burns, bullet and shrapnel injuries, and some had arms and legs amputated. Welsh Guardsman Simon Weston, OBE, badly burned in *Sir Galahad,* endured more than sixty operations. His extensive burns became the face of courage and suffering of so many so long afterwards. He was welcomed back to the Falklands to receive the Islanders' gratitude. Helped by marriage and fatherhood, he formed a UK charity called the Weston Spirit to help disadvantaged teenagers and wrote a children's book. He personifies man's enduring spirit and will to live.

Rick Jolly continued to research post-traumatic stress disorder (PTSD), from which many veterans of all wars suffer. It causes mental problems, nightmares and vivid flashbacks of the horrors of war and dying comrades. PTSD has caused many veterans, both British and Argentine, to commit suicide.

Rick Jolly, the surgeon who saved so many, could not himself be saved by his surgeons. He died from heart trouble in 2018, aged 71.

25

ISLANDERS AT WAR

Threats fail to quell defiance and sabotage.

During occupation, Islanders endured bullying, threats, curfews, restrictions, arbitrary arrests and incarceration, as well as extreme danger trapped between forces locked in battle.

They came under bombardment from bullets, shells and low-level bombing. Many houses were damaged. Some were deliberately burned down by Argentine soldiers. There was no place to hide in such a small town as Stanley, less than a mile long and half-a-mile wide, dotted with Argentine trenches, armoured vehicles and machine gun emplacements. Islanders described it as 'hell on earth'. Astonishingly, only three civilians, all women, were killed, ironically by a misdirected British naval shell.

Argentina's pledges to respect Islanders' rights proved worthless, as my despatches explained at the time:

Argentine television pictures show the normally near-deserted streets of the tiny capital patrolled by amphibious armoured vehicles and steel-helmeted soldiers all over the place. The contrast comes as a shock. Previously the British uniformed police of six men and one woman were the only arbiters of law of what little crime there was in what was one of the most peaceful places on earth. The only sounds came from sheep and wildlife, from the multitude of penguins and seabirds. The head of the Roman

Catholic Church on the Islands, Monsignor Daniel Spraggon, said: 'It will take a long time before we get back to the peace and tranquillity. Our people have never soldiers in the streets.' The postmaster, Bill Etheridge, whose colourful Falklands wildlife stamps are sought the world over by collectors, said: 'My family have lived here for one-hundred-and-fifty years. After all that time the boundaries of the world should not be withdrawn. I am still British.'

The Argentines promised the Islanders they would be free to continue their way of life in harmony and peace. But they would be regarded as Argentine citizens. Empty promises gave way to restrictions interfering in daily life. The military tried to impose Argentine stamps, driving on the right of the road not the left, banned listening to the BBC and confiscated radios and aerials, including the inter-island communications sets so valuable on isolated farms, removing the means to keep in touch with their children and with neighbours, or call for help in emergencies.

As well as the governor and senior officials, the Argentines evicted Islanders they considered troublemakers. The official left in charge of the community was the treasurer, Harold Rowlands. A feisty, truculent Islander, he rejected a demand to convert to Argentine currency, mischievously declaring: 'I cannot change from pounds to pesos because, at my age, I cannot handle all those noughts!' Inflation in Argentina had been astronomical.

The Argentines restricted freedom of movement with curfews confining Islanders to their homes, threatened them with prison for disobeying their diktats and up to sixty days' jail for 'showing disrespect' for the occupation forces. I reported the Islanders' risky defiance:

The sturdy Islanders with a reputation for toughness and fortitude seem largely to have ignored the strictures. They have been walking about as usual and honking their car horns when they pass Argentine soldiers. They keep asking Argentine reporters trying to interview them, 'When are you going home?' The Islanders are fiercely clinging to British customs. They have always rejected Argentine influence and the Spanish language. General Menéndez said English would be accepted until educational reforms were brought in and the Islanders learned Spanish.

26

IMPRISONED IN COMMUNITY HALLS

Terrifying ordeal. Locked up and facing death threats.

Goose Green residents were imprisoned in the community hall. The 115 detainees, fearful of their fate, included forty-three children and two people over 80 years old.

Argentine soldiers had rounded them up from their homes, leaving no time to get coats. At first, they had no food or bedding and only two toilets.

They were warned that if anyone tried to leave, they would be shot. In breach of the Geneva Convention governing warfare, the building was not marked as housing civilians. They were not provided with shelters against air and artillery bombardment. They lifted the floorboards to dig dank, uncomfortable bunkers for safety.

The Goose Green civilians were massed at the heart of the Argentine defences as a human shield.

Convinced their prisoners were transmitting radio messages, the Argentines carried out searches which included everyone, even 4-month-old Matthew McMullen. As detailed by Graham Bound in his book, 'They would look in his nappy while the watching adults hoped Matthew had a special surprise for them!'

They were kept in the hall for a month as food ran short. Catholic priest Monsignor Daniel Spraggon remonstrated with the Argentines to relieve their plight.

Dozens of Stanley's citizens were also rounded up and incarcerated in Fox Bay community hall. These included Velma Malcolm, who described her arrest with characteristic bluntness: 'A big burly bumptious bugger said: "You're going to Camp." He had drawn his pistol and was standing over me.'

Richard Cockwell waged psychological warfare, emerging on bitterly cold mornings in a flimsy vest and shorts. Running on the spot to divert attention from goose pimples, he would greet the Argentine sentry, cowering from the cold, with a cheery, 'Good morning. What a lovely warm day. Wait until winter comes!'

Many other hostages were locked up in farms at Goose Green, Pebble Island and Fox Hill. An Islander told how he was threatened on the porch of his house by an Argentine with a gun. He was accused of being a spy and transmitting information to the fleet. He was pushed flat on his stomach, face down, with his hands tied tightly behind his back. He was left there all day while the battle was going on.

The Argentine who caused most fear was the sinister head of military police intelligence, Major Patricio Dowling. He had personal dossiers on Islanders and carried out arbitrary house searches and arrests. At Neil and Glenda Watson's Long Island Farm, Dowling pointed a weapon at their young daughter, Lisa, and repeatedly ordered her to stand up. Lisa repeatedly said no, and continued sucking her thumb.

Some Argentines treated the Islanders sympathetically. Comodoro Carlos Bloomer-Reeve did a great deal to protect Islanders from the excesses of his colleagues. He was amiable, always smiling, not politically driven, having previously lived in Stanley with his family, and made friends with Islanders when he ran the Argentine air force passenger service to the Falklands. Naval Captain Barry Melbourne Hussey was another Argentine with humane principles. These two officers showed fundamental decency and responded to calls from Islanders to defuse dangerous situations.

Heavy, badly driven armoured vehicles churned up roads and knocked down fences. Islanders' homes were vandalised and possessions stolen. Their vehicles and bicycles were requisitioned. The dairy herds and chickens were slaughtered for meat.

Inexperienced, ill-equipped conscripts suffered from cold, hunger and combat fatigue. When captured by the British, they were allowed to sleep in sheds full of food that their officers had not distributed. Frozen food unloaded from ships had been left to rot on the quayside. One conscript who had not taken off his boots for two months said a British soldier carried him piggy-back to a stretcher. His frostbitten feet were a bloody mess with the stench of rotting flesh.

27

ISLANDERS FIGHT BACK

Women led front-line fighting farmers. 'Rubber Duck' and radio ham heroes.

The Islanders engaged in active resistance and gave vital help to the advancing British troops. They risked danger, deportation and imprisonment, carrying out sabotage, spying on military activity, transmitting intelligence by radio, ferrying ammunition to the front line and the wounded back to safety, guiding advance patrols, and fighting in the front line, expertly exploiting their experience of rural fieldcraft.

Astonishingly, Professor Freedman's government-funded lengthy three-volume account of the conflict found no space for the Islanders' valiant contribution to their own liberation. That is an omission for which he offered no meaningful explanation when I asked him why.

I was standing next to Margaret Thatcher in the Falkland Islands when she urged that their story should be told. So, the Professor's omission was made good in a book, *Falkland Islanders at War*, by one of their own, Graham Bound, a journalist and founder editor of the *Penguin News* newspaper. He describes in riveting detail their ordeal and their deeds of derring-do, which they also later told me about in many interviews.

Women, as well as men, were in the forefront of 'the fighting farmers', as they became known. The Islanders had unrivalled driving skills, used to such rough terrain.

Frontline fighters

Two Islanders – former police chief Terry Peck and aircraft engineer Vernon Steen – were awarded British medals for their bravery fighting in the front line in the ferocious close-combat battle for Mount Longdon.

'Rubber Duck' takes off

Some of the most daring adventures were undertaken by Terry Peck, described as 'a tough, gutsy maverick', who became a legend. In the initial stages of invasion, he walked about, pretending to be back in his old job as a plumber, carrying a length of drainpipe concealing a telephoto camera identifying military targets which he smuggled to British intelligence officers.

To avoid arrest, he fled Stanley on a motorcycle. He laid low for ten freezing days and nights in the open. He once avoided capture by hiding in a locked toilet where his Argentine pursuers could not flush him out! Caked in mud, he arrived at Trudi Morrison's Brookfield Farm, where she insisted he take a bath and threw a child's toy at him, saying: 'You have forgotten your rubber duck.' This became his codename. He carried a skilfully forged identity card altering the letters of his name from 'Terry Peck' to 'Jerry Packer'.

Farmer Neil Watson helped him find weapons on Long Island beach buried by the British Marines detachment before they surrendered. Armed with rifle, ammunition and grenades, Terry Peck set off by motorbike to meet the advancing British troops, already being guided from their San Carlos beachhead by 14-year-old Saul Pitaluga on his motorbike. Terry Peck passed on vital information and maps of Argentine positions and guided advance patrols led by Major Pat Butler to Mount Longdon, stealing stealthily past Argentine patrols, even on moonlit nights.

Peck, 44 years old with only territorial training, fought side-by-side with the paratroopers who elected him as one of their own as an honorary member of the regiment, complete with their coveted red beret. In the victory parade through Stanley, he proudly marched as their right marker.

He was stunned by the ferocity and brutality of the battle for Mount Longdon, as men bayonetted men in close combat, with the dead and dying littering the mountaintop.

Reverting to civilian life, he would gaze in the peace and quiet of his lounge in Stanley upon distant Mount Longdon, with the sun reflected by a steel cross monument at the summit, as he relived the horrific memories of war. He died comparatively young, from cancer. Ironically, his son, Jamie, later emigrated to Argentina, married and had Argentine children.

The quiet engineer

Vernon Steen, an NCO in the volunteer Falkland Islands Defence Force, joined Terry Peck as a guide on Mount Longdon, scouting ahead with an advance patrol to penetrate the Argentine defence and capture soldiers still in their sleeping bags. He guarded the equipment of Sergeant Ian McKay VC, killed as he assaulted a mountaintop machine-gun nest. Vernon Steen's soldierly qualities in war were masked by his modesty in peace. He returned quietly to Stanley to begin rebuilding the Falklands Air Service, whose aircraft the Argentines had destroyed. He never mentioned the carnage he witnessed on Mount Longdon.

'Undisputed woman leader'

To get ammunition and supplies up the mountains, Terry Peck suggested they exploit the Islanders' tractors, trailers and cross-country driving skills. He radioed Trudi Morrison: 'Rubber Duck here. Can you get as many drivers and vehicles together as possible and meet us at the Heathmans?' Tony and Ailsa Heathman at Estancia Farm provided shelter and food for the 600-strong Para battalion, for which they received no recognition.

In response to the request for help, Trudi declared: 'There is no way I am going to miss this. I am doing my bit for my country.' Described as 'the undisputed leader', driving her Land Rover, she gathered a wagon train with drivers from every farm in the area. Her partner, Roddy McKay, drove an old, incredibly noisy caterpillar tractor, which came under attack from an Argentine Skyhawk.

From Johnson's Harbour came Bruce May and Claude Molkenbuhr; from Rincon Grande, Keith Whitney; from Port Louis, Trevor Browning and Andres Short; and from Green Patch, Raymond Newman, Pat Whitney, Maurice Davis, Terry Betts, Mike Carey and Peter Gilding. They were joined by brothers Patrick and Ally Minto and Terence Phillips from Mount Kent.

Major Roger Patton praised their resourcefulness, determination and courage. He said the troops could not have managed without them. Major Pat Butler said he had the deepest respect for them.

Trudi distributed the tasks to the tractor teams, who, with little sleep, moved 300 paratroopers, rations, ammunition and water across trackless terrain, in driving rain, to their tactical position on Mount Estancia, shuttling supplies around-the-clock, under attack from Argentine artillery, mortars and bombing. As the battle raged, the civilians evacuated badly wounded soldiers back to helicopters at Teal Inlet.

Trudi Morrison (later Trudi McPhee) was highly praised in a commendation from the Commander-in-Chief, Admiral Sir John Fieldhouse:

> On 11 June, she drove a Land Rover in support of the 3rd Battalion the Parachute Regiment operation to secure Mount Longdon. Travelling across the most appalling terrain, without lights, she drove one of only three Land Rovers which success-fully arrived at the mortar line. At times under enemy artillery, Mrs Morrison resolved to continue, showing tremendous stead-fastness in dangerous and unfamiliar circumstances.

The Admiral's tribute hardly begins to describe the terrifying, seemingly endless ordeal of that night for which, surprisingly, Trudi was not awarded a medal.

Skilful tractor driver

Philip Miller, as a very young man, was praised by the Paras on Mount Longdon for driving the tractors and sledges carrying missiles. His uncle, Tim Miller, was later wounded when shrapnel from a Harrier bomb attack destroyed his sight in one eye.

Radio ham hero

The Cape Pembroke lighthouse keeper and former British Antarctic Survey radio expert, Reg Silvey, turned his hobby as a radio ham into a weapon of war, transmitting intelligence to Britain at great risk from his stone cottage, defying an Argentine ban enforced by radio detector vans. His Falklands call sign, 'Victor Papa Eight', was picked up by Bob North, a radio ham in Rotherham, Yorkshire.

Silvey fooled the Argentines by handing in a spare radio smuggled to him by George Betts, captain of the *Monsumen* supply ship. He dismantled his conspicuous normal aerial, adapting a brilliantly simple substitute, his steel core washing line stretched across his garden, and illegally acquiring a notice signed by the Argentine governor, General Menéndez, denying entry to Argentine soldiers. It said: 'his house had been cleared by the military police'.

He indulged in dangerous spying, sending fifteen-second bursts of intelligence about Argentine gun emplacements and ammunition supplies at Stanley airport that could be attacked as there were no Islanders there. His dangerous work was never officially acknowledged.

'Castrating' communications

Veterinary officer Steve Whitley and teacher Phil Middleton indulged in 'dangerous mischief', cutting army telephone wires with his vet's castrating scissors and taking clandestine photographs of Argentine defences. Steve Whitley's young schoolteacher wife, Susan, along with two elderly Falklands women, Doreen Bonner and Mary Goodwin, were killed and Steve and others seriously injured in John Fowler's house by a misdirected British naval shell from HMS *Avenger*. Susan is buried in a wildlife haven she loved, Sea Lion Island, and her memory is kept alive by an annual school essay competition for generations of children born long afterwards.

When Robin Pitaluga, Saul's father, on Salvador Farm used his radio to try to pass a message from the task force to the Argentines to surrender, heavily armed men were helicoptered in to arrest, interrogate and terrorise him with a mock execution, holding a revolver to his neck and pulling the trigger without his knowing it was unloaded. He was tied up in a trench overnight then put under house arrest.

Denzil Clausen was beaten up because the Argentines thought he was transmitting messages when he was only tuning in to the BBC World Service. Other radio hams at Port Louis – Chilean Mario Zuvic Bulic, Andres Short and his father – intercepted, confused and jammed Argentine signals. Eileen Vidal, who manned the radio telephone system, relayed military intelligence to HMS *Endurance,* warning Captain Barker to keep away from Stanley, as it was crammed with Argentine warships.

Islanders rendered government vehicles unserviceable. On invasion night, Canadian immigrant Bill Curtis tried to redirect the Argentine aircraft beacon and was arrested. Goose Green farm manager Eric Goss and others hid petrol and immobilised tractors to deny their use to Argentines, as well as sabotaging water pipes that servied the invaders. When the Argentines asked about lights in the distance indicating British patrols, Eric made up the on-the-spot fiction that they were a curious local phenomenon – moonlight reflecting on seaweed-covered rocks at low tide!

Electricians Les Harris and Bob Gilbert cut off Argentine power supplies and inserted low tolerance fuses to halt transformers serving the military. Public Works Department head Ron Bucket and his staff maintained essential services for the Islanders, for whom plumbers led by Dennis Paice and Derek Rozee kept water supplies flowing. The men who maintained the electricity and water services were described as 'local heroes', as was 19-year-old Constable Anton Livermore. The volunteer fire brigade, organised by Lewis Clifton and Neville Bennett, made valiant, exhausting efforts to quell fires and save buildings from burning down.

Keeping Islanders safe

Education Superintendent John Fowler evacuated children to safety from Stanley. Des King and his family sheltered Islanders in their Upland Goose Hotel. The Falkland Islands Company manager, Terry Spruce, offered West Store as a reserve shelter. He and his store manager, David Castle, provided food, comfort and understanding, for which they were highly praised by Islanders who found the ladies' millinery department 'a calming environment'. Safe houses were marked out for civilian refuge, equipped with short-wave radio to receive BBC World Service.

Parents worried about the psychological impact and trauma of hostile military occupation on impressionable young children. Yet Argentine conscripts were given food by compassionate Islanders.

Caring doctor and peace negotiator

Dr Alison Bleaney, with her baby gurgling in the background, supervised essential medical services and was instrumental in arranging the Stanley ceasefire, for which she was awarded the MBE.

Resourceful Deputy Governor

Rex Hunt paid tribute to his deputy and Chief Secretary, Dick Baker, for his cool, pragmatic reaction and organised leadership, going around Stanley on invasion night as bullets were flying indiscriminately. Dick Baker was a reassuring presence, an expatriate official totally trusted by the Islanders, living among them in the community with his wife and two young daughters. He was later appointed Governor of Saint Helena.

Heroes all

It is surprising more Islanders were not awarded the medals their courage deserved. Several did receive certificates of commendation by Admiral Fieldhouse for their bravery. But the awards were few and their unrecognised deeds many. It was another thirty-three years before the Queen awarded a collective South Atlantic Medal to the Islanders in recognition of their assistance to the task force.

Decades later, cruise ship tourists, guided to penguin colonies by the Islanders, had no idea they were in the presence of civilian war heroes and heroines, driving their four-wheeled vehicles with the same consummate skill in peacetime and in daylight under the penguins' benign gaze and not Argentine guns. And they volunteer their services, vehicles and their homes to welcome British veterans revisiting the battle sites.

GOING HOME

Counting the cost. Widescale damage. Menace of deadly hidden mines.

The task force left the winter snow and storms for a rapturous midsummer welcome. Ships bedecked with flags and bunting sailed into their home ports as crowds sang 'Rule Britannia'. It was a hero's return.

By contrast, Argentine troops were repatriated as prisoners of war, defeated, demoralised, and largely ignored by the Argentine public who had so vociferously praised them on invasion day. This was no hero's welcome. Argentina was, as one journalist described it, 'The Land that lost its Heroes.' The truth of how Argentine soldiers were brutally treated by their own commanders was revealed only decades later.

Argentina's cruelty to its own front-line troops was a hidden atrocity. The ordeal of ill-educated, ill-trained conscripts was aggravated by horrific, humiliating abuse and ill-treatment by their own officers and non-commissioned officers.

Documents kept secret until 2015 revealed how they were beaten, given electric shocks, raped and deliberately starved, losing half their body weight. Four conscripts died of starvation, and two others were shot dead.

Conscripts foraged in residents' bins for leftover food. Leaving their trenches to salvage rotting animal carcasses or trap and slaughter farm animals brought severe punishment from well-fed officers, who ordered that they be shot for forcibly taking food from Islanders, many of whom had given them food out of compassion. Nazi-sympathising officers singled out Jewish conscripts for severe punishment. They were ordered to urinate on fellow Jewish conscripts and kneel with hands tied behind their backs to eat like pigs from a pit dug as a communal toilet. They were thrown into a hole to languish for hours in frozen water.

Some were staked out, crucifixion style, on sodden, peaty ground in freezing weather for as long as ten hours, losing consciousness and close to death from hypothermia. One conscript was forced to hold a hand grenade in his mouth for two hours by a sadistic officer who stole their food. The head of the army, Lieutenant General Cristino Nicolaides, excused the abuse as 'disciplinary punishment'.

Former soldiers, bullied to keep silent, plucked up courage after thirty years to launch a legal case, backed by 700 pages of declassified testimonies, accusing at least seventy officers and non-commissioned officers of crimes against humanity. Traumatised teenage conscripts regarded their own officers as their worst enemy rather than the professional, disciplined British forces, whom they were exhorted to fight for 'a glorious cause'.

The conflict had wide-ranging consequences. Britain gained international prestige. Argentina's once all-powerful armed forces lost power and were cut drastically.

The Falklands' limited infrastructure had been overwhelmed by the 10,000 Argentine invaders, who left behind an unedifying mess – all the detritus and unhygienic filth of war. They left a less visible but more menacing, long-lasting legacy of 25,000 unexploded anti-personnel and anti-vehicle mines in 117 minefields, as many as 1,300 mines within a one-mile diameter on one mountaintop. Their presence desecrated the pristine pastures, farms, beaches, sports grounds, children's play areas and barbecue venues – a dangerous and selfish denial for the post-war generations.

Several British soldiers had their legs and feet blown off, stepping on mines. The minefields were cordoned off with barbed wire and skull and crossbones warning signs. Children were taught of the dangers and how to recognise mines. They were all enrolled as 'Bomb Disposaleers' in an imaginative campaign of education by Royal Engineer bomb experts.

Removal of the mines was a near-impossible task, hindered by wintry weather and boggy terrain in which plastic mines could not be located by metal detectors nor exploded by flails mounted on vehicles which only drove the mines deeper into the ground. Some floated out to sea and were deposited on beaches elsewhere. And some were 15 metres deep under sand dunes.

Under the 1997 international mines-ban convention, it was the UK's responsibility to get rid of the Falklands mines, which cost the British taxpayer £44 million. The UK employed the expertise of an international company of experienced de-miners from Zimbabwe to carry out the dangerous, painstaking task, often working waist-deep in mud and water or sinking into sand dunes burying mines several feet deep.

More than thirty-eight years after they were laid, the Islands were declared free of mines in November 2020, a historic milestone meaning that all British territories worldwide were free of landmines.

The Zimbabwe team spent eleven years in the Islands, earning them high praise and the gratitude of the Islanders for, as one legislator said, 'giving us back our home and allowing us to roam freely again'. They were relieved of the ever-present fear of stepping on a mine. Hundreds of Islanders celebrated as the last mine cordons were taken down. They swarmed onto previous no-go areas, jumping for joy and splashing into the waves.

Several of the Zimbabweans settled in the Falklands for a better life and brought their families, a total of fifty in all. They all got employment, and their children were educated for free.

Another 2.8 million items of ordnance, ranging from bullets to bombs, also had to be removed. Civilian casualties were mercifully avoided, and wildlife barely suffered. Thousands of penguins sat happily undisturbed in the minefields, too light to set them off. The absence of human activity meant that once-popular beaches were taken over by penguin colonies.

The Islanders reacted with pragmatism, living with the mines routinely in their daily lives. For years, farmer Leon Marsh drove every day down a narrow track between minefields that dissected his farm of 8,000 sheep at Fox Bay. Mr Marsh said: 'The landmines became a way of life.'

Unselfishly, the Islanders said priority should be given to other countries where mines had killed or injured hundreds of thousands of people, as in Afghanistan and Cambodia. On their farm in West Falkland, Roger and Norma Edwards had 4,000 acres strewn with landmines. Mrs Edwards, a former nurse, said: 'Countries where children have to walk through minefields should have priority. Put us on the end of the list.' Roger Edwards fought in the war as a Royal Marine attached to an elite SAS unit. In peace, he and his wife became legislators campaigning worldwide to preserve hard-won freedom from Argentine claims.

The UK government pledged another £36 million for removal of mines elsewhere in the world, estimated at more than 110 million.

Argentina had delayed mine removal for years, arguing over whose responsibility it was.

29

CHILE INVASION AVERTED

Chile next target. Argentina planned war to seize Beagle Channel islands.

An immediate, far-reaching but unknown consequence of Argentina's defeat is that its military regime was forced to abandon a secret plan to invade Chile.

It was more than thirty years later that Galtieri's former air force chief, Brigadier Lami Dozo, revealed that Argentina had made preparations to wage war on Chile to seize three disputed islands at the tip of South America. The brigadier said this would have been a regional war with calamitous casualties.

It would also have shattered a peace accord brokered by Pope John Paul II, which averted such a war in 1978. The Pope's compromise awarded the Beagle Channel islands to Chile, in line with arbitration by the International Court of Justice in 1977.

I reported Argentina's renewed threat in a BBC despatch on 22 January 1982:

Argentina has renounced peace treaty with Chile on their Beagle Channel dispute over three islands and the surrounding seas potentially rich in oil … The dispute has soured relations for years and brought them to the brink of war in 1978 … War was averted only by last minute intervention by the Pope whose compromise peace plan has now been rejected by Argentina …

Argentina says the Pope's compromise breaches a century-old bi-ocean principle that what's in the South Atlantic is Argentina's and in the Pacific is Chile's. Both countries have spent thousands of millions of dollars in a big arms build-up.

Margaret Thatcher expressed gratitude to President Augusto Pinochet for Chile's invaluable help to the British task force. To her chagrin, she was unable to prevent his prolonged detention during a visit to Britain as a result of an international arrest warrant issued by a Spanish prosecutor accusing him of human rights crimes.

30

WHO WAS TO BLAME FOR FALKLANDS CONFLICT?

Official report clearing UK government is ridiculed as a 'whitewash'

After the war, exhaustive official inquiries came up with contradictory conclusions. The Thatcher government was controversially cleared of any blame for the conflict by an independent official inquiry led by a former government official, Lord Franks. But a mass of evidence contradicts its findings. Its key conclusion was: 'We would not be justified in attaching any criticism or blame to the Government for the Argentine junta's decision to commit its act of unprovoked aggression in the invasion of the Falkland Islands.'

The Franks inquiry was not required to attribute blame to individuals, but had to consider any 'failures in the machinery of government'. Its members were entirely establishment figures – two retired senior civil servants (Lord Franks and Sir Patrick Nairne) and four former ministers, two of them Conservative (Lord Watkinson and Lord Barber) and two Labour (Lord Lever and Merlyn Rees).

Critics questioned whether that membership could really be described as 'independent'. The inquiry's terms of reference required it 'to review the way in which the responsibilities of Government were discharged in the period leading up to the invasion'. This focus on the immediate pre-invasion period virtually ruled out criticism for the policies and acts of successive governments, both Conservative and Labour, for nearly two decades.

Even the head of one of those governments, former Prime Minister James Callaghan, damned the Franks report as a 'whitewash'. He was also a former Foreign Secretary in Harold Wilson's Labour government, which initiated negotiation with Argentina on sovereignty as early as 1965, at the behest of the United Nations.

The Franks inquiry's findings were challenged by many dissenting voices, the most influential of which was the all-party House of Commons Foreign Affairs Committee. Its wide-ranging investigation in 1985 declared that warnings of potential Argentine military aggression were ignored. It delivered a damning indictment of the government, declaring that there were:

> so many acts of omission when the warnings and indications and risks had been so clear. The invasion cannot be properly described as coming 'out of the blue' … Events showed an extraordinary lack of co-ordination between the Ministry of Defence and the Foreign Office, who had accurately predicted both the risk and the course of events as early as October 1979 [a few weeks after Mrs Thatcher became Prime Minister]. Lord Carrington appeared to do everything possible to keep *Endurance*. The evidence given to the Franks Committee shows very clearly that it was primarily the Prime Minister and Mr Nott who made the wrong decisions and that their degree of culpability has not been sufficiently recognised.

The Foreign Affairs Committee had no doubts that there was 'failure of government'. It said the very survival of the Prime Minister may have been at stake. Accusing the government of political motives, the Foreign Affairs Committee declared: 'The Government had committed thousands of men and a large part of the Royal Navy not just to retake the Falklands but also to protect and secure the life of the administration. It became a political imperative to recover the Islands.'

The Chairman of the eleven-man Foreign Affairs Committee, Sir Anthony Kershaw, was a Conservative loyalist with unrivalled experience as a lawyer, a former army officer honoured for gallantry, and a Member of Parliament for thirty-two years serving as a minister at both the Foreign Office and the Ministry of Defence. Other committee members included eminent lawyers and long-serving MPs. Their conclusions carried convincing weight.

31

INVASION WARNINGS IGNORED

Sleepwalking to war. Invasion scenario predicted in 1975 and 1979 intelligence alerts.

The Foreign Affairs Committee challenged Margaret Thatcher's claim that she had virtually no warning of the invasion and no intelligence until too late for countermeasures. This is simply untrue. Intelligence warnings stretched back several years and intensified in early 1982.

There were ominous signs of aggressive intent by the junta, influenced by an explosive domestic environment. In London, there was an incomprehensible lack of awareness or military preparation.

There were warnings aplenty from British official intelligence reports, from Argentina and from Falkland Islanders who came back from visits to Argentina convinced the junta intended to invade at the end of March. The Deputy Governor and Chief Secretary, Dick Baker, said to me that efforts to sound alarm bells in London were wasted. 'A lot of us did foresee it. The tragedy was no one in London seemed to want to know or to react to the signals … Why nothing happened in response is a great mystery to me.' He suspected there was a deliberate policy to ignore the signals and to weather an invasion in the hope that Britain would be rid of a troublesome colony. 'We used to joke we were expendable,' said Dick Baker.

This is a serious indictment from a respected senior official at the centre of events. But it accords with the determination of the Foreign Office to be rid of the colony and placate Argentina. Dick Baker, who courageously rounded up Argentine residents on the eve of invasion, reacted with 'disbelief' to the Franks Committee's findings, which he derided as 'ridiculous'.

Scathing criticism came from a knowledgeable naval officer, Captain Nick Barker, commander of HMS *Endurance*, who spent years patrolling the South Atlantic. He accurately assessed Argentine intentions and its incursions into British territory such as the South Sandwich Islands as 'predatory'. His warnings to London were dismissed as a captain's campaign to save his ship from the scrapheap. Captain Barker called the Franks Committee's findings an 'appalling whitewash'.

To those of us in Buenos Aires, it had seemed that British politicians were on a different planet and the two countries on a collision course. Invasion speculation was rife in Argentine newspapers. The editor of the English-language newspaper the *Buenos Aires Herald*, James Neilson, a politically acute Scot, said:

> it became clear that Argentina was contemplating invasion four months before it happened. We tried to persuade the Foreign Office in London it had a serious problem, either to build Fortress Falklands to avert invasion or negotiate sovereignty. The Foreign Office took the comfortable course of pretending nothing had changed. The blame does really lie in London, not Buenos Aires.

A well-informed Argentine journalist, Iglesias Rouco, writing in *La Prensa*, which had close contacts with the navy, warned that if Britain did not accept Argentina's proposals, the junta might resort to force, which might enjoy United States support. Rouco said Britain had no more than four months to acknowledge transfer of sovereignty by January 1983, the 150th anniversary deadline. Rouco predicted direct military action between the middle and the end of 1982 (which accorded with the junta's original secret timetable).

In a BBC despatch on 26 February 1982, entitled 'Invasion Speculation', I quoted a Foreign Ministry spokesman as saying: 'Argentina's patience is running out and the new Galtieri government wants "quick results" [on surrender of sovereignty].'

British Embassy diplomats monitored newspaper reports, as did the BBC Monitoring Service in Caversham for analysis by the Foreign Office and MoD. Two senior military attachés – an army colonel, Stephen Love, and a naval captain, Julian Mitchell – said they faced difficulty trying to monitor military movements in such a vast country.

Yet, as a journalist refused a residence permit or press credentials by the military, I travelled to the Andes to see mountain troops facing Chile, and to the far south to the port of Ushuaia to witness frenetic naval activity. Clues were signposted in the public domain by the Argentines themselves. UK Foreign Office policymakers failed to recognise the warnings or deliberately ignored them as an Argentine ploy.

Warnings about Argentina's intentions went back not just weeks but years. As Prime Minister nearly thirty years before the invasion, in 1953 and 1954, Winston Churchill vetoed the sale of helicopters to Argentina when his military chiefs told him Argentina could successfully launch a surprise invasion

In succeeding years there was a spate of intelligence warnings.

Warning Number One: Argentina had for years publicly emphasised its January 1983 deadline by which it demanded action. It reiterated this in mid-1981 in a Foreign Ministry document.

Warning Number Two: As early as November 1975, Harold Wilson's Labour administration was alerted by the government's Intelligence Committee that 'a deliberately planned invasion in the near future seems unlikely but could not be wholly excluded'. In fact, an invasion plan had been under detailed discussion by Argentine officers in the early 1970s.

Warning Number Three: Secret Argentine occupation of the isolated Island of Southern Thule in 1975 (the first step in its long-term clandestine strategy 'Project Alpha') was described by the UK government's Intelligence Committee as 'a political and physical demonstration of sovereignty' and might encourage more such Argentine landings.

Warning Number Four: In October 1979, soon after Thatcher became Prime Minister, Lord Carrington sent a memorandum to the Cabinet's Defence Committee declaring that 'a Fortress Falkland' policy or talks without making any concessions on sovereignty would both carry a 'serious threat of invasion', and that if Argentina saw no progress, there would be 'a high risk of its resorting to more forceful measures including direct military action'.

Warning Number Five: In November 1979, the Joint Intelligence Committee (JIC) updated its assessment declaring that:

> while the Argentine Government would prefer to achieve their sovereignty objectives by peaceful means, if negotiations broke down or if for some other reason the Argentine Government calculated that the British Government were not prepared to negotiate seriously on sovereignty, there would be a high risk of their resorting quickly to more forceful measures ... direct military action against British shipping or against the Falkland Islands could not be discounted.

Carrington acknowledged in mid-1981 that 'the sands were running out' for reaching agreement.

Warning Number Six: In July 1981, the Intelligence Committee reiterated its view that 'military action could not be ruled out if by early 1982 the Argentines concluded that Britain would not negotiate'. That precise scenario was reached on 1 March 1982 when the Argentine government signalled its view that there was no serious negotiation on sovereignty. The invasion was then fewer than five weeks away.

Warning Number Seven: A British colonel is quoted as saying that, on a visit to Argentina, he was warned a year beforehand of an invasion, and shown amphibious personnel vehicles that Argentines told him would be deployed in the invasion.

Warning Number Eight: Lack of progress in the New York Anglo–Argentine talks on 26 and 27 February meant, as the Foreign Affairs Committee investigation pointed out, that 'the serious threat of invasion predicted by the Foreign Office in 1979 had arrived'.

Warning Number Nine: On 2 March, the military attaché in Buenos Aires, Colonel Love, envisaged the Argentine navy landing marines on the Falklands, and if the Argentines believed a negotiated settlement was no longer possible, there might be 'a straight seizure of the Islands'.

Warning Number Ten: The next day, 3 March, after receiving a telegram from the British Ambassador in Buenos Aires, Thatcher scribbled on it, 'we must make contingency plans'. This would still have given time, a whole month, to send warships and submarines to deter or intercept the Argentine invasion armada, but her instruction was not carried out. Submarines were subsequently ordered south but too late.

Warning Number Eleven: Not long before the invasion, the Prime Minister received an intelligence report declaring 'without equivocation an Argentine invasion seemed likely in the early hours of 2 April'.

A contradictory intelligence briefing the same day said that 'deploying further units in the circumstances, which were potentially no more serious than on many previous occasions, indeed less so in view of the forthcoming talks (on sovereignty), would have damaging effects on our other commitments' (to NATO).

In a written warning in December 1981, for distribution to all BBC news editors, I said Argentina was determined to take action on what it called 'recovery of the Malvinas' by January 1983. This was not prescient speculation on my part, as the previous Foreign Minister, Oscar Camilión, had issued a document in mid-1981 publicly declaring: 'Our principal foreign policy in 1982 is to recover sovereignty of the Malvinas.' Six weeks before the invasion, I was refused interviews with General Galtieri because he was 'too busy' reviewing his troops in the south of Argentina. Military bases there would be the launch pad for the invasion.

The Foreign Minister, Doctor Costa Mendez, refused me an interview, but I was permitted to interview the Head of the Malvinas and Antarctic Department, Señor Blanco. I asked point-blank: 'Do you intend to invade?' He spluttered an unconvincing 'No!' – but he gave me another copy of the 1981 Foreign Minister's statement, which emphasised the priority for 'recovery of the Malvinas' by January 1983.

The same day, at the British Embassy, the ambassador, Anthony Williams, was hosting a reception for a joint Anglo-Argentine military climbing expedition which had scaled a volcano in the

Andes. Amid the celebrations and clinking of glasses, the ambassador turned to me and said: 'See the camaraderie. Relations have never been better between our two countries!' At that moment, preparations were well advanced for the invasion. The ambassador's remark was surprising as he was involved in the attempts to defuse the threatening crisis. It was later revealed that his sympathies lay with Argentina, to the extent that there were allegations that he betrayed the United Kingdom by withholding vital information from Lord Carrington.

SECTION THREE:
THE MEDIA
AND THE WAR
OF WORDS

32

RIVETING RADIO COMMENTARY

Live phone-in links Islanders and governor.
Brave broadcaster rebukes gun-wielding soldiers.

Radio was a vital source of news, not just worldwide but also for Islanders who listened to BBC reports from Buenos Aires, London and the task force.

Closer to home, they were glued to a remarkable all-night invasion broadcast by the head of the Falkland Islands Broadcasting Service (FIBS), Patrick Watts, in a unique feat of public broadcasting. In peacetime, Patrick was renowned for his sporting and horse racing commentaries. This was a different, deadly scenario, a graphic blow-by-blow account of invasion, tracking the advance of hostile forces.

Patrick's marathon transmission became a fascinating 'phone-in' with many Islanders joining in, as did the governor, who ordered Patrick to stay on the air to keep the population informed and relay vital advice and authoritative assurance. Patrick, the father of two young daughters, took a swig of brandy to steel him for the ordeal ahead.

Islanders called in describing what they could see outside their front windows – troops and tanks with Argentine flags. One caller remarked: 'I can see the stars.' Patrick told him: 'For goodness' sake don't stay outside. Get inside.' The man responded: 'No, I am looking through a hole in the roof.'

At 9 a.m., Patrick heard the thud of boots and six soldiers burst into the studio, pointing guns at his back. Patrick told them to stop shouting and put out their cigarettes. Over the airwaves, he uttered the most momentous words of his career. 'Stop that racket. Will you take the gun out of my back? Take the gun away. I am not speaking with the gun in my back.' How is that for British phlegm in a moment of crisis, defying excitable trigger-happy troops who might just press the trigger?

Remarkably, the Argentines obeyed. Patrick was determined to keep a British presence on the air as a vital conduit of information and advice to save lives. Some listeners complained when he welcomed a ceasefire. He told them: 'It is good news that a truce has been agreed. If nobody gets shot, the better it is. I do not want any of our local lads who are hopelessly outmanned to be shot and wounded.'

The Argentines requested tapes be played saying what the invaders wanted. Patrick, calmly, without histrionics, told his listeners: 'The radio station has now been taken over by the Argentine invasion force. His Excellency the Governor is on the line now.'

In his autobiography, Governor Rex Hunt describes his confrontation as the Argentine Marines Special Forces Commander, Admiral Carlos Büsser, enters Government House:

> I told the Admiral he had landed unlawfully on British territory and I ordered him to leave forthwith. He refused, claiming he was taking back territory that belonged to Argentina. I said it was reprehensible that Argentina should have seized the islands by force after Britain and Argentina had agreed at the UN to settle the dispute by peaceful means. He appealed to me to cease the

needless bloodshed as he had an overwhelmingly superior force. I said I cannot argue with that. I would not have agreed to a ceasefire if we had anything like comparable forces.

The Governor praised the bravery of the British troops and continued broadcasting: 'The Admiral gave an assurance that no Islanders would be harmed in any way. I said that some of his troops had already broken into Islanders' homes. He immediately told his second-in-command to discipline the wrongdoers.' The Governor signed off: 'This is probably the last message I shall be able to give you. I wish you all the best of luck, and rest assured, the British will be back.'

Patrick Watts kept broadcasting throughout the occupation alongside English-speaking Argentine broadcasters. He maintained his subtle defiance, altering the propaganda 'news' and exploiting music as a weapon.

When Argentine commands became so confusing that even their own soldiers did not know what was supposed to be done, Patrick raised a few smiles with humour and a hint of mockery by wryly playing over the radio 'When the circus came to town'.

He left his post only to be with his family towards the end when the British bombardment intensified. He returned on the morning of the surrender. 'It was like someone flicked a switch and everything stopped. No more noise. The studio door was wide open. The place was in darkness. The Argentines had just walked out and I never saw them again.'

Patrick went on air and played 'Land of Hope and Glory' and 'God Save the Queen'. He told the relieved Islanders: 'You are listening to the Falkland Islands Broadcasting Station. No longer LR60 Radio Nacional Las Malvinas.' He remarked later: 'It was great to say that. It really, really was.'

Patrick's brave demeanour was a precursor to practical and psychological sabotage by the Islanders and their help to British troops. He epitomised the character of the Islanders – tough, brave and never kowtowing to anyone, least of all an Argentine, and definitely not an Argentine with a gun. He was awarded an MBE for his courage and stamina.

His invasion-night marathon was an impressive piece of public broadcasting in unique circumstances. It was preserved for posterity thanks to the presence of mind of his assistant, Myriam Booth, to record the whole phone-in on tape. Patrick smiles as he recalls the trauma and reflects on the irony that the war opened the way for a more successful Falklands.

Another Islander, John Smith, kept a remarkable day-by-day and sometimes hour-by-hour diary of the occupation lasting seventy-four days, which he published in a book. It is a fascinating insight into the thoughts, actions and fears of a people under siege.

33

CHALLENGE TO MEDIA

Journalists flock to Buenos Aires, face jail threats and censorship. Others go to sea, then war, bombed, shelled and freezing.

For journalists working in Argentina during military rule, these were dangerous times. We felt safer in the glare of publicity from the Falklands conflict when more than 700 journalists from around the world congregated in Buenos Aires – but they also faced threats, restrictions and frustration from a regime waging a propaganda campaign as well as a war. Journalists were confined to the capital and barred from travelling south to the war zone 1,000 miles away. They had no access to first-hand, impartial information but only to tainted military sources. They, too, relied on radio bulletins for news.

Three British journalists – Simon Winchester of *The Sunday Times*, Ian Mather of *The Observer* and his photographer, Tony Prince – defied the travel ban and travelled to Southern Argentina. They were arrested in the most southerly town in the world, Ushuaia, where they monitored the conflict in their cells on BBC radio, as Simon Winchester testified in his *Prison Diary*.

A state of emergency and censorship prohibited reports on the weather in the South Atlantic, the firepower of the British forces, and 'any military information except from official sources'. Communiqués gave the junta's version of events. Television carried martial music and images of Argentine troops and weaponry giving the impression of power and invincibility, and stressing the theme of 'unity and patriotism'.

Radio Rivadavia, a station allied to the regime, blared out from loudspeakers in the streets. 'Malvinas Anthem', introduced with a bugle call and a roll of drums, was played repetitively, with the chorus '*Todos juntos a cantar, Malvinas Argentinas*' ('Altogether now, the Malvinas are Argentine').

The junta banned publication of news from abroad and 'all information on military matters affecting national security' or 'causing panic, disunity or contradicting official information'. The BBC was on a hiding to nothing!

The communiqués advised Argentines to ignore rumours, untruths and false expectations to avoid what they called a British psychological campaign to undermine Argentine resistance. Breaches of these vaguely defined restrictions could involve closure of publications and detention of their directors.

Censorship proved unworkable. The BBC's freedom of the airwaves gave it a long reach, not just to Simon Winchester's prison cell but to all corners of the globe. Its reports were rebroadcast by many foreign stations. I received several death threats, was harassed in the streets, arrested twice, and had six policemen in three shifts monitoring my movements day and night for three months. During six years of military rule, more than 120 journalists 'disappeared', which meant they were kidnapped and murdered, and many others were jailed.

One journalist who survived imprisonment was Jacobo Timerman, whose son, Héctor Timerman, subsequently became Foreign Minister when civilian rule returned. Jacobo Timerman wrote a book called *Prisoner Without a Name, Cell Without a Number*, words which capture the helplessness and isolation of his solitary confinement. He was allowed only one visitor, his rabbi, Marshall Meyer, who befriended me and kept me informed of his ordeal. The Rabbi offered me sanctuary in his synagogue from kidnap gangs, but I declined. The synagogue was a target of the military's Nazi-style hate campaigns, daubing swastika signs on its walls. In those dangerous days, there was no place to hide in Argentina or elsewhere.

Robert Cox, editor of the *Buenos Aires Herald*, one of the most courageous and conscientious journalists, repeatedly challenged the regime and championed the disappeared and their grieving relatives. He was forced by death threats to quit Argentina when he learned of a plot to kill him in a street shootout. He telephoned me to say he was leaving overnight for the United States with his Argentine wife and five children. The Interior Minister, a cynical general named Harguindeguy, sarcastically told Bob Cox that if everyone who received a death threat left Argentina, the country would be empty. Another *Buenos Aires Herald* editor, Andrew Graham-Yooll, escaped by the back door of the newspaper offices as a military kidnap squad entered through the front door.

I was warned by aides of General Albano Harguindeguy that, along with an American *Newsweek* journalist, if we tried to visit a beach where bodies were being washed up, our bodies would be among them. We didn't go.

The frustrations for the media in Buenos Aires were nothing compared with those of journalists with the task force, regarded at first as the favoured few. The Prime Minister's Chief Press Officer, Bernard Ingham, overcame opposition from ministers and military commanders for journalists to accompany the task force, a total of twenty-nine chosen from 160 applicants. They included newspaper, news agency, television and radio reporters and photographers. They were regarded by the navy as a nuisance and a hindrance. No foreign media were permitted.

Filing from the front line, at sea and on land, they were dangerously exposed to bombing, shells and foul weather, ill-prepared for the rigours of war, with no winter clothing. They faced censorship and frustration as they fought their own war of words with irritated commanders and Ministry of Defence censors, who had total control of communications. The journalists accused these 'minders' of deliberate obstruction and delaying tactics in an atmosphere of mutual antagonism.

They faced almost insuperable logistical and transmission obstacles. To file reports on satellite links from merchant vessels, correspondents were forced to beg for helicopter lifts from ship to ship or shore to ship, braving high winds and heavy seas as they were winched down onto heaving decks. Sometimes reports entrusted to helicopter pilots 'got lost'.

Five influential reporters arrived at the action very late. For nearly two weeks, they were left bobbing about at sea, at first in an ammunition ship crammed with explosives, then in a decoy vessel deployed to attract missiles away from the warships. The 'Invincible Five', as they became known, were in danger of being blasted to oblivion by bomb attacks. They represented the cream of journalism: John Witherow (*The Times*), Alfred McIlroy (*The Daily Telegraph*), Gareth Parry (*The Guardian*), Tony Snow (*The Sun*), and Michael Seamark (*Daily Star*). They spent much of this time listening to the BBC World Service.

The most successful and prolific journalist, Max Hastings (*London Evening News*), later an experienced military historian, established a remarkable rapport with the armed forces, displaying tenacity and initiative. To the chagrin of his fellow journalists, his opportunism earned him fame as the first media man to stride into Stanley with the advance troops as it was being liberated.

Television journalists Brian Hanrahan (BBC) and Michael Nicholson (Independent Television News) faced formidable obstacles caused by bad weather, lack of communication facilities, MoD non-cooperation and censorship, enabling it to control and manage the news. Television videotapes shipped to Ascension Island were forwarded by a broadband satellite link, with delays of up to three weeks – longer than it took reports of the Charge of the Light Brigade in the Crimean War in 1854 to reach *The Times* from its correspondent, William Howard Russell!

There were no photographs for the first fifty-four days and television exploited stock footage with correspondents' voice-overs. Hanrahan described what it was like:

> On ship it was possible to shut out the threat of air raids and go on writing. On land it was not. You go into a trench and stay there for hours. You have to set up your own camp, cook your own food and dig your own trench in cold and dangerous sur-roundings … Restraint and restrictions slowed and diminished our reporting. Bad news was instinctively delayed.

BBC radio reporter Robert Fox described his difficulties:

> Much of the campaign passed in a whirl of hitching lifts in heli-copters, seizing boats to ply to stormy anchorages, impersonating all ranks, high and low, to get the vital transfer to the ship with the right kind of satellite telephone … A remarkable feature was the

amount of walking, and two units, 3 Para and 42 Commando, virtually walked the breadth of East Falkland, 50 miles. The column
of march would be 2 miles long. Routine orders and messages
would be passed from man to man.

Radio emerged as a vital communications tool as well as a
morale booster for the Islanders.

34

PROPAGANDA FAILURES

War of words as well as weapons. MoD's 'McDalek'. Pathetic 'Operation Moonshine'.

In London, Ministry of Defence news was controlled by television announcements by their acting Chief of Public Relations, Ian McDonald, delivered in a dull, mechanical monotone which mesmerised the public and earned him celebrity status and the nickname 'McDalek'.

The civilian head of the MoD, Permanent Secretary Sir Frank Cooper, gave confidential press briefings and admitted he did not always tell the whole truth or correct mistakes so as to deceive the Argentine military.

The government introduced a Spanish language propaganda programme, *Radio Atlantico del Sur* (South Atlantic Radio). This was the brainchild of the MoD Special Projects Group (SPG) to conduct psychological warfare operations, known in military jargon as 'Psyops'. Its unfortunate codename was 'Moonshine', which the sceptical, blunt-spoken Bernard Ingham criticised as 'playing downmarket, dirty propaganda tricks'. Admiral Fieldhouse was similarly unimpressed.

It was judged by Professor Lawrence Freedman's *Official History* to have been 'hastily conceived, belated, botched and costly' and spectacularly ineffectual. Its aim was to 'persuade Argentine conscripts to surrender with minimum resistance'.

It would broadcast 'truthful' information on the conflict, 'reducing dependence on wildly inaccurate Argentine claims'.

The BBC was not to be involved in order to protect its independence and integrity. The station purported to be neutral from another country. The MoD requisitioned one of the BBC's four transmitters on Ascension Island, weakening its audibility and its ability to counter Argentina's jamming, so it had to double its wavelength frequencies.

Radio Atlantico del Sur broadcast commentaries, sports items and even record requests that claimed to come from Argentine mothers for their sons in the Falklands but were obviously fictitious. The station carried pro-British news and reports damaging to Argentina. It told the Argentines that British rifles and machine guns were so powerful they could penetrate walls!

British newspapers derided the station as banal and unprofessional with 'sentimental ethnic music' from Mexico unfamiliar to Argentines, and its Spanish as ungrammatical, delivered by university-educated British civil servants in clipped formal style in Chilean and Colombian accents. The BBC christened it 'Ascension Alice' and criticised its 'commercial radio style bordering on the vulgar'.

The Times was scathing in an article headlined: 'The Ultimate Weapon – Radio Station could be the last straw for Invaders'. It declared that if British artillery, RAF raids and appeals for peace did not cow them into submission; it was just possible the 11,000 Argentine troops would surrender just to get away from *Radio Atlantico del Sur* and its sheer awfulness.

The Argentines did not even try to jam it. When I asked General Menéndez what he thought of it, he replied: 'I never heard of it.' Neither had his senior intelligence officer. Menéndez said he did not listen to the BBC but Uruguayan Radio, which he did not realise rebroadcast BBC programmes.

The Argentine front-line conscripts whom *Radio Atlantico del Sur* was designed to demoralise had no radios. The cold, hungry conscripts were already demoralised, as they described in their letters home to their families, contradicting jingoistic government claims of their high morale. The propaganda station broadcast for less than a month for five hours a day until the surrender – forty-seven broadcasts, costing the British taxpayer £40,000.

Another UK propaganda ploy was to shower Argentine soldiers with leaflets emphasising their vulnerability, together with Good Conduct passes and appeals to surrender. But it proved logistically impossible to fire the leaflets from fast-flying jet planes.

The Argentines had their own propaganda broadcasts. When they expropriated Falklands Radio, they renamed it 'Radio Liberty' (LR60 Radio Nacional Islas Malvinas), and put Buenos Aires TV news anchor Silvia Fernández Barrio, known as 'Argentine Annie', on the air. General Menéndez made broadcasts exhorting his troops to fight to the last man *por la patria* (for the nation).

Propaganda was interspersed with music: tango for the Argentine troops, and country and western for the Islanders. The Argentines introduced a new medium, television, previously non-existent in the Islands. They established 'Canal Siete' (Channel Seven) and sold a shipment of TV sets to locals on easy-hire purchase, which they snapped up, correctly assuming that they would never have to complete the repayments. Argentine 'news-propaganda' was mixed into the schedule of old films, *Fawlty Towers* videos and *Tom and Jerry* cartoons. A Roman Catholic minister gave nightly addresses mixing religious with patriotic messages. But Argentine troops had no access to it.

An *Argentine Gazette* was issued promising to tell the troops the truth. To boost morale, it told them how valiant they were, just as good soldiers with just as good weapons as the British. As the British advanced on Stanley, General Menéndez broadcast a desperate rallying call, declaring: 'The enemy will be destroyed by the decisive action of each one at his combat post ... Victory is certain ... *To arms! To battle!*'

Futile rhetoric was reinforced again by resorting to religion and the Catholic Church. The *Gazette* announced: 'The Military Government was placed under the protection of the Blessed Virgin Mary in her dedication as Our Lady of the Rosary of the Reconquest and Defence.'

Propaganda by both sides proved to be futile.

35

BBC'S UNIQUE ROLE

Government takeover threat. BBC denies 'irresponsibility' and 'treason'. Defends its patriotism.

Government ministers, Members of Parliament, and military commanders were critical of British media coverage in general and the BBC in particular. Thatcher complained of 'even-handedness' and 'chilling neutrality' for referring to 'British troops' and 'Argentine troops' instead of 'our boys' and 'the enemy'. The BBC was abiding by its own long-established guidelines, saying, 'We should try to avoid using "our" when we mean "British".' It was not its job to boost the morale of British troops. The Director-General, Sir Ian Trethowan, said the BBC must be sensitive to the emotional sensibilities of the public.

Margaret Thatcher accused the BBC of letting down the armed forces, the country, and her. A book entitled *Pinkoes and Traitors* by Westminster University Professor of Media Studies Jean Seaton, the BBC's official historian, says that the Home Secretary, William Whitelaw, came under 'immense pressure' to take control of the BBC to direct what it broadcast. Whitelaw deflected this threat. Instead, he arranged a meeting between the BBC executives and the Conservative Parliamentary Media Committee, who vented their fury at the BBC's acting Director-General, Alasdair Milne, and chairman, George Howard.

Margaret Thatcher complained that the BBC exaggerated the views of the war's critics and of 'a few dissidents voicing Left-wing propaganda'. The BBC pointed out that thousands of its staff were routinely vetted by the security services to deter any threat to national security by extremist views.

BBC Defence Commentator Peter Snow faced fierce criticism, as did current affairs television programmes, especially *Panorama* and *Newsnight*, for analyses and speculation by military experts, so-called 'armchair generals'. The lack of task force television footage led to reliance on readily available film and comment from Argentina. Conservative Members of Parliament described one *Panorama* programme as 'odious and repugnant'.

The BBC resented accusations of 'treasonable behaviour' and the slur on its patriotism, saying it could not be neutral and even-handed between Britain and an aggressor. It would not be exactly impartial, just as, in the Second World War, it took Britain's side. But it would be 'truthful' to protect its worldwide reputation for 'objectivity and reliability'.

It avoided such dismissive words as 'Argies', though tabloid newspapers had no such scruples. The two main tabloids took opposing viewpoints. The *Daily Mirror* was anti-war, while *The Sun* indulged in 'Argie-bashing' and jingoistic headlines, of which the most notorious were 'Stick It Up Your Junta' and 'Gotcha' when *Belgrano* sank with heavy loss of life.

Government ministers and military commanders accused the BBC World Service of 'aiding the enemy' by revealing ship and land force deployments.

Brigadier Thompson said: 'I am absolutely fed up with hearing my plans broadcast on BBC news.' Commodore Clapp 'seethed with anger' when Nott revealed his ship deployment plans on the World Service, 'losing the advantage of surprise and damaging morale … BBC reports could have exposed the 5th Infantry Brigade reinforcements on *Canberra* and *Norland* as easy submarine targets.'

This was a particularly vulnerable phase of the conflict, as Admiral Woodward angrily pointed out:

> The BBC had blown our cover, announcing to the world that the Battle Group and the Amphibious Group had joined up. I had hoped that this could have remained a military secret until after the landing but, as ever, the British media were more interested in the truth than for the consequences for our own people.

The press, he said, were not 'on our side … Argentine generals and admirals gained 90 per cent of all their intelligence about our activities from the British press. BBC World Service was particularly helpful (to the Argentines). The Director-General should be charged with treason.'

The Admiral criticised what he called 'shallow, smug, half-educated morons at the BBC. Their self-appointed task of fearless seekers after the truth was, to them, sacrosanct. It may have been paid for by the blood of Captain Hart-Dyke's people [in HMS *Coventry*, nineteen of whose crew were killed and David Hart Dyke was badly burned].' The World Service had reported that Argentine bombs aimed at warships were not exploding.

Admiral Woodward conceded that the Argentine commanders themselves may have sorted out the bomb-fusing problem. He was grateful to be given film shot by BBC cameraman Bernard Hesketh of HMS *Sheffield* after the Exocet missile attack, which was 'very useful' to him. The BBC and ITN made available all their film, both broadcast and unused.

The BBC World Service came in for more criticism for predicting the imminent attack on Goose Green before it had begun, indicating the position of the British parachute battalion. The Paras unfairly directed annoyance at Robert Fox, who carefully avoided any speculation damaging to the troops whose dangers he shared.

In fact, the report was based on briefings by the Ministry of Defence and John Nott himself. Colonel H. Jones threatened to sue the Ministry, John Nott and Thatcher.

General Moore suggested Nott had revealed 'the timing, axis of advance and objectives'. He requested that 'Ministry of Defence press officers delete mention of units and movements. Sorry if this denies politicians the pleasure of moving pins on their *Child's Atlas of the World*.'

Admiral Sir Terence Lewin thought it likely the Argentines had anticipated an attack in time to reinforce the Goose Green garrison. Post-war analysis by Professor Freedman in his *Official History* blames John Nott and Ministry of Defence briefings. He concluded that the BBC report had little impact on Argentine reaction, as they expected an attack on Goose Green.

The BBC's positive influence is given scant recognition in the *Official History*. UK opinion polls indicated wide public support for BBC reporting and for standing up for Britain above all other media.

Despite so much criticism, BBC broadcasts earned praise and respect for influencing world opinion in Britain's favour and for sustaining the morale of the Falkland Islanders, as confirmed by a cable to the BBC Director-General, copied to me, from the leader of the community during the occupation:

Telegram to BBC Director-General, 1982

FROM: Harold Rowlands, most senior Government official during occupation.

'Throughout the Falklands crisis, there was continuous praise here for the BBC Services. The BBC was the only reliable news media to inform us what was taking place in the Islands and the South Atlantic. Reception was good and we wish to thank producers, announcers, technicians, and other contributors for their magnificent coverage.

'A special word of thanks to Harold Briley for keeping us informed of events in Argentina. There is no doubt he was outstanding. Finally, many thanks to all who participated in producing *Calling the Falklands*.'

Rex Hunt, the governor most involved in support of the Islanders, also praised the BBC's role and thanked me for my broadcasts in his autobiography *My Falkland Days*, saying:

There was no one in Buenos Aires who had a more helpful attitude to the Islanders than Harold Briley … The most comforting voices to the Islanders were those of the British Ambassador to the United Nations, Sir Anthony Parsons, and Harold Briley's. He did a terrific job keeping up morale. The Falkland Islands expressed their appreciation with a huge banner saying 'God Bless you, Harold'.

British newspapers acknowledged the BBC's unique ability to communicate with the beleaguered Islanders and transmit 'messages of hope' voiced by family, friends, government ministers, Rex Hunt, the Archbishop of Canterbury, and even the Queen.

Calling the Falklands, a programme broadcast weekly for sixty-four years, became essential listening and greatly extended its transmissions. They were anchored by a veteran presenter, Peter King, who endeared himself to Islanders, signing off with his comforting catchphrase, 'Heads down, hearts high.'

Ironically, twenty-five years later, this radio lifeline fell silent, axed as it was no longer needed in the new media world of satellite television and mobile phones. Its archives were lost, including much of its historic invasion coverage.

BBC English- and Spanish-language programmes were rebroadcast by other stations, augmenting the BBC's own world-wide audience of 120 million. The chief commentator in Spanish, Chilean Domingo Valenzuela, won many listeners for his interviews rebroadcast by dozens of Latin America radio stations. Millions of Argentines tuned in to BBC English and Spanish news.

Even Argentina's spokesman in Buenos Aires, a senior naval captain, who daily briefed hundreds of international journalists on the junta's version of the fighting, asked to join me to listen every night on my radio to the BBC World Service.

BBC reports were credited with shortening the war and saving hundreds of lives, civilian and military, by persuading Argentine commanders of the futility of fighting on. They asked broadcaster Patrick Watts for a daily summary of BBC reports.

BBC radio news of the British advance and the crumbling Argentine cordon around Stanley persuaded the Argentine commanders to defy Galtieri and surrender, according to both British and Argentine sources. A British army intelligence officer declared this was the case, as did the Argentine military chaplain, Padre Salvador Santore, who said reports from the BBC, Uruguay and Chile were believed, in preference to what were regarded as 'suspect' reports from Argentine media.

Tributes flowed in for outstanding coverage by Robert Fox and Brian Hanrahan, described even by Thatcher as an 'excellent correspondent'. His famous 'I counted them all out and I counted them all back' quote was considered by Admiral Lewin as 'justifying, on its own, all the press hassle before and after'.

The BBC Relay Station in Ascension Island, led by Resident Engineer Norman Shacklady, played a vital support role to the task force in overcoming logistical obstacles. And its transmitters frustrated Argentine jamming of BBC broadcasts.

Islanders defied threats of punishment to continue listening. Those incarcerated in the community halls in Goose Green and Port Howard hid their radios under floorboards and shoved their aerials out of windows on broomsticks when their guards were not watching as they sheltered from the wintry weather.

Since the conflict, British Forces Broadcasting has provided radio and television services to the Falklands garrison and the civilian population. And the long-established Falklands radio broadcasting service has been joined more recently by a private initiative television programme founded by Islander Mario Zuvic Bulic.

For me, reporting such a historic event was personal, as many of the Islanders were my friends. They have welcomed me back many times since.

36

MEETING THE ISLANDERS

Anticipating trouble in the BBC's biggest 'patch'

The BBC had shown little interest in Latin America as a source of news. I was the only staff correspondent stationed there, with no support staff, to cover 8 million square miles and thirty diverse countries, including Mexico, Central America, the Caribbean, and all of South America from Amazonia to Antarctica. Most were military governments hostile to the BBC.

Geography, poor communications, travel obstacles, corruption, bureaucracy, and the Latin American *mañana* mentality frustrated rapid deployment to get to the right place when news broke.

An invaluable source of news for me was Reuters news agency and its correspondents, totally reliable wherever I worked in the world.

In my reconnaissance trip to the Falkland Islands in January 1981, my reports captured a snapshot in time of an unspoilt, tranquil backwater before it was inundated by a military tsunami.

As key figure, the Governor, Rex Hunt, was an impressive diplomat, sympathetic to the Islanders. He told me: 'They are more British than the British. They remind me of my own folk back in Yorkshire.' But the UK's policy favouring Argentine sovereignty made them suspicious, as he could not readily confide in them on what was happening.

His area of responsibility was vast, as he explained to me: 'I am Governor of the Falkland Islands, South Georgia and the South

Sandwich Islands, High Commissioner of the British Antarctic Territories and Commander-in-Chief, British Forces, Falkland Islands. I am responsible for 1,800 people, 600,000 sheep and 6 million penguins!' Uniquely, his official car was a red London taxi which, he said, 'is the only vehicle into which a colonial governor in feathered headgear and a dangling sword can step without falling over!'

The Islanders were friendly and hospitable, hard-working and self-reliant. They were no drain on the British taxpayer. They sent back to the UK more money from the farms to absentee landlords and companies than any UK finance received by them.

A support lobby in London led by a barrister, Bill Hunter-Christie, mobilised opinion in favour of the issues and later became the Falkland Islands Association.

I interviewed Thatcher on an RAF flight to the Falklands and told her she should not be so critical of the BBC. She was unaware that its broadcasts in Russian during the Cold War had prompted the Soviet Union to brand her 'the Iron Lady', an accolade in which she rejoiced, enhancing her personal image and political success. She later visited the World Service to thank its broadcasters for their role in winning 'the Cold War'.

Throughout the Argentine occupation, I broadcast a special personal 'Letter of the Air' every week on *Calling the Falklands.* I chatted to the Islanders as old friends, reassuring them that Britain was on their side. It was far from orthodox BBC or the 'neutral approach' which annoyed Margaret Thatcher. In appreciation of BBC broadcasts, I was made an international honorary life member of the Falklands Club known as 'The Gluepot'. It allows me free drink for life twenty-four hours a day, with my own front door key! It is a long way to go for a free drink.

SECTION FOUR: 1982–2022 RECOVERY AND AFTERMATH

37

FORTRESS FALKLANDS – OR IS IT?

Could it happen again? Is airbase vital for rapid reinforcement vulnerable?

To deter Argentine aggression, rapid air reinforcement via Ascension Island became possible with the new post-1982 air and military base at Mount Pleasant, 35 miles from Stanley. The UK's aircraft carriers and their jump-jet Harrier aircraft were scrapped in 2010 and not replaced until 2020 – by new giant carriers with the most modern warplanes.

Some military commanders speculated that the airbase remained exposed to sudden capture, leaving reinforcements nowhere to land. Admiral Lord West, captain of a warship, *Ardent*, sunk in the conflict and later a Labour government Security Minister, argued that cuts to British armed services aggravated the vulnerability of the Islands to Argentine action. But the UK has been greatly strengthening the Royal Navy by building a new generation of modern warships, including frigates.

Argentina has re-equipped its forces with modern weapons, including a 2021 order for multi-role warplanes from Pakistan and supplementing more French Super Étendard aircraft which caused such damage to the 1982 task force. Successive civilian governments insist they won't resort to force, but a future military government might do so. In the meantime, the armed forces, an all-powerful influence that have been significantly reduced since 1982, have maintained a low political profile.

The UK is sure that any attack can be repulsed with its formidable defence resources patrolling the seas, a garrison of troops, and protection from air attack with warplanes, radar stations and anti-aircraft Rapier missiles. RAF and chartered airliners maintain regular flights from the United Kingdom. There are air-sea rescue services with which the Queen's grandson, Prince William, did a duty tour with the RAF.

The UK rejected Argentina's accusation of 'militarising' the South Atlantic, as deterrent defence was needed to counter Argentine threats.

38

OIL IN TROUBLED WATERS

Oil discoveries boost Falklands prosperity, enrage Argentina.

More than two centuries ago, in 1770, the writer Doctor Samuel Johnson, arguing against going to war with Spain over the Falklands, dismissed the Islands as 'thrown aside from human use … Stormy in winter, barren in summer which not even the southern savages have dignified with human habitation.'

How wrong he was! Since 1998, offshore oil and gas discoveries have promised wealth beyond imagination, though there have been many delays in going ahead with production. Drilling by local and giant international companies has been influenced by fluctuating oil prices.

Oil and gas could add hundreds of millions of pounds to the Falklands' revenue. The British firm, Rockhopper, found oil worth billions of dollars near Sea Lion Island, 75 miles (120 kilometres) offshore. Rockhopper was transformed by a multimillion-dollar investment from Premier Oil, a worldwide operator.

It was the forerunner of several multimillion-dollar partnership deals. Falklands Oil and Gas (FOGL) attracted substantial investment from the United States Company, Noble Energy, and from Edison International, an Italian subsidiary of the French group, EDF.

Falklands Director of Mineral Resources Stephen Luxton welcomed the deals as a vote of confidence by the industry. New ports will handle supply vessels. Falklands firms benefitted from the construction of infrastructure and accommodation for oil workers.

Any oil in Falklands waters belongs to the Islanders. But they promised a contribution of oil revenue towards their defence, which has cost about £60 million annually.

The Islands impose stringent safety standards to prevent oil spillage and safeguard their unique environment and wildlife. Oil would not be piped ashore but ferried from platforms at sea by tankers to destinations elsewhere.

These discoveries exacerbated the territorial dispute. Argentina claimed ownership of oil and other resources in what it called 'the Argentine continental shelf', which it greatly extended in 2020 by 650,000 square miles, encompassing the Falklands and all other British territories in the South Atlantic and Antarctic, as well as all resources in the sea specifically targeting fisheries and oil. Its laws threaten fishery and oil firms with jail and fines, and confiscation of ships, drilling platforms and bank accounts. But Argentine domestic laws are not recognised as valid internationally. Oil companies dismissed the threats, saying the industry deals with political disputes all around the world.

The United Kingdom supports the Falkland Islands' right to develop their natural resources in accordance with United Nations Conventions of the Law of the Sea and on Civil and Political Rights.

Argentina threw away an opportunity to share in Falklands oil operations provided by a co-operation agreement with President Carlos Menem (1989–99). His Foreign Minister, Dr Guido Di Tella, made strenuous efforts to woo the Islands in what was called his 'charm offensive'.

Later governments ended all co-operation on oil development and on conservation of fish stocks.

Argentina imposed restrictions on charter overflights travelling to the Islands and on shipping traversing Falklands and Argentine waters, including fishing vessels. The United Kingdom denounced this as 'intimidation and blackmail' breaching the UN Convention on the Law of the Sea (UNCLOS) to provide right of innocent passage and freedom of navigation.

Argentina has persisted with its claim to sovereignty in campaigns throughout Latin America, the European Union and in the United Nations, whose Special Committee of twenty-four, known as the 'Decolonisation Committee', debates the dispute every year.

The United Kingdom says: 'There can be no negotiations on sovereignty unless the Islanders so wish based on the principle and right of self-determination in the UN Charter and the International Covenant on Civil and Political rights.'

The most aggressive President, Cristina Fernández de Kirchner, faced charges in the courts of links with corruption. But she was shielded from prosecution as a member of Congress and returned as Vice-President in 2019.

Twelve years of confrontation were interrupted briefly between 2015 and 2019 with the election of the centre-right government of President Mauricio Macri, previously Mayor of Buenos Aires. He promised better relations and co-operation on economic issues, trade, fishing, shipping, oil and regional air links. All these policies were abandoned by the next government of President Alberto Fernández in 2020.

39

THE MODERN FALKLANDS

Self-governing democracy. Unprecedented prosperity. Flourishing new and old industries.

All peoples have the right to self-determination. By virtue of that right they freely determine their political status and freely pursue their economic, social and cultural development.
– United Nations Charter

The Falkland Islanders, like all people, claim that right. In a land-mark referendum in March 2013, the Falkland Islanders voted to stay British, by a landslide 99.8 per cent majority. They called it 'a democratic, incontestable' rejection of Argentina's sovereignty ambitions.

Argentina disputed the referendum result, saying that the Islanders are *not* a 'people' qualified by the UN Charter.

The Islanders, who have implemented democratic political reforms, say:

We value our constitutional links to the UK, founded on free choice. Our home is not a colonial relic but a vibrant twenty-first century democracy. We are our own community, free to determine our political future. The more Argentina presses our small community, the harder will be our resolve. We favour co-operation and peaceful co-existence.

The political status of the Falkland Islands, by their own choice, is as one of fourteen UK Overseas Territories guaranteed the right of self-determination, security and good governance. South Georgia and the South Sandwich Islands, also claimed by Argentina, are a separate British Overseas Territory. The Falklands elect their own eight-member Legislative Assembly responsible for domestic affairs. A governor is appointed by the UK, which retains responsibility for defence and foreign affairs.

Members of the Legislature lead an international campaign at the United Nations and globally to assert their rights. A Falkland Islands Government Office (FIGO) in London has won strong support from parliament, the public, and the media. FIGO is headed by the Government's Representative, who acts like an ambassador.

The Islanders have created a thriving, dynamic nation, fulfilling the forecast by Rex Hunt that they would demonstrate, by their conduct, their gratitude to the British forces, 'whose suffering and sacrifice shall not have been in vain'. Fittingly for a former Spitfire pilot, Sir Rex adopted Winston Churchill's immortal tribute to the Royal Air Force on the Battle of Britain by declaring: 'Never before in the field of human conflict was so much owed to so many by so few!'

The Falklands have become one of the richest countries in the world per head of population. They have encouraged immigrants from Saint Helena, also in the South Atlantic. Most inhabitants live on the two main islands, East and West Falklands, with 85 per cent in the capital, Stanley. There are 740 smaller islands, most uninhabited.

Reconstruction with UK aid was a colossal task. Power, water and sewage services had collapsed. There was no bakery, laundry or pier for unloading supplies. From the destruction of war,

Stanley has been transformed. The Islanders have enjoyed full employment, high living standards and low taxes. There is virtually no crime or drug taking.

The architect of prosperity was Lord Shackleton, son of the legendary explorer Sir Ernest Shackleton,[1] who visited the Falklands in 1916 after surviving his epic trans-Antarctic expedition. After the 1982 conflict, Lord Shackleton updated his 1976 proposals to revive the flagging economy. I accompanied him on his second mission, which brought about radical reforms providing more roads, a bigger school and airport. Government grants enabled tenant farmers to buy their own land, splitting up large farms previously owned mostly by the Falkland Islands Company (FIC). This company had dominated commercial activity since its formation in 1851 and owned nearly half of all the land in the Islands until Shackleton's reforms. It continues to play a dominant role, providing many other services.

Shackleton's masterstroke led to declaration of a conservation zone of about 200 miles around the Islands in 1986 to create a fishing industry that transformed the economy. It brought in tens of millions of pounds annually from foreign vessels, mainly from Spain, Taiwan, Korea and Indonesia, to exploit waters teeming with squid, hake and other species. Islanders created thriving fishing companies and fleets of their own.

---

1   The achievements of the two Shackletons are commemorated by the Shackleton Scholarship Fund (SSF), founded by a former Governor, David Tatham, to award scholarships for South Atlantic research by eminent academics and quality-of-life scholarships to experts in the arts, music, sport and other activities to share their knowledge with Islanders, who also qualify for scholarships abroad to broaden their experience.

An outstanding entrepreneur, Stuart Wallace, married to an Argentine, was one of the Cable and Wireless employees who tried to send the invasion night alert to London. His story illustrates the invaluable contribution Islanders have made to their own success, with energy, enterprise, creating opportunity and jobs for the younger generation.

He became one of the Falklands' leading businessmen from modest beginnings, having left school aged 15. While working in various jobs, he was elected the youngest legislator in the Falklands government and in any British territory worldwide. As a legislator and member of the post-war Development Corporation, he helped to rebuild the Islands' infrastructure, then formed a fishing company in partnership with the other Cable and Wireless technician, John Cheek, who tried to send the invasion message in 1982.

Their firm, Fortuna, has prospered, with several vessels catching squid and toothfish, leading the way with scrupulous standards of sustainable fishing.

But UK exit from the European Union created obstacles to access for Falklands fishery exports to its main lucrative market in the EU in co-operation with Spain and other European enterprises. Despite tariff obstacles, the fishery industry continues to flourish, with modern vessels enhancing catches.

Agriculture, based on traditional sheep farming, continues to produce high-quality wool, and the Islanders restocked their dairy herd, slaughtered for food by Argentine troops. A modern abattoir produces meat for Islanders, the British garrison, cruise ship passengers and for export. Lambs from sixty farms increased tenfold.

Organic methods flourished using minimal fertiliser. Vegetables were grown commercially in Stanley's large hydroponic market garden. Wind power, readily available in such exposed islands surrounded by ocean, generates electricity even for the power station. Farms have their own pylon windmills, a business developed by a former shepherd, Clive Wilkinson, originally from Croydon. Peat, previously used for heating and cooking, has been superseded.

Conservation and research measures have protected fish stocks so that seabirds and marine life were not deprived of essential food. The Islanders led a campaign to prevent widescale drowning of albatross caught on longline trawler hooks. The Natural Resources Director for many years, John Barton, won international acclaim for one of the best-regulated fishing regimes in the world.

A recent enterprise was the creation of a South Atlantic Environment Research Institute (SAERI). In 2021, a Falklands Environment Trust was formed to facilitate donations from oil and other companies to compensate for any damage to the environment. Maritime Management Zones protect wildlife and sustainable fishing.

The Islands' wildlife is a magnet for the tourist industry. Visitors stay in modern hotels, guest houses and farm lodges. In normal times, until the virus pandemic, tens of thousands of day-trippers would go ashore from more than fifty cruise ships every season. The Falkland Islands Government Air Service (FIGAS) provides flights throughout the Islands, some of which are also linked by ferry. The virus pandemic caused an interruption of cruise ship visits and flights from Brazil and Chile, with stops in Argentina.

All Falklands' basic industries, impacted by the pandemic, were protected with emergency government grants paid from large reserves built up in prosperous times.

Priority is given to the protection of the Falklands' prolific wildlife, which includes giant elephant seals, dolphins, whales and sea lions. Among more than 200 species of birds is the largest colony of black-browed albatross in the world, nesting in their tens of thousands.

Falklands Conservation, a charity protecting wildlife, employs high-tech modern methods to monitor penguins' well-being. Five species of penguins include the colourful, majestic king penguin, towering above the whiskered rockhopper, Magellanic, gentoo, and macaroni, a fascinating attraction to visitors.

Tourists flock to a thriving king penguin rookery, a few miles from Stanley at Volunteer Point, part of a 10,000-acre nature reserve, named after a visit by a ship called *Volunteer* in 1815. It is accessible from Stanley by four-wheel drive vehicles, which take several thousand cruise ship visitors there each year.

It had a modest beginning when two king penguins waddled ashore and took up residence on a sheep farm. The colony multiplied from thirty pairs of king penguins in 1971 to 2,000 pairs of adults with 860 chicks in 2020, joined by their smaller cousins – 1,800 pairs of gentoo penguins and a similar number of Magellanic penguins. They forage far out to sea for food.

World-class trout fishing has attracted tourists and pleased even the Duke of Edinburgh on his visit.

The wildlife is a paradise for photographers and naturalists, though the greatest of naturalists, Charles Darwin, was not impressed on his visits in 1833 and 1834 on his voyage of the *Beagle*, encountering bad weather.

The winter war of 1982 gave a false picture of the climate, which is temperate, with moderate rainfall, sometimes scorching sun, and persistent strong winds. The weather can be very variable, sometimes providing 'all four seasons in a single day', as the Islanders say.

Stanley has expanded with many new buildings but its skyline is still dominated by the most southerly Anglican cathedral in the world, Christchurch, fronted by a unique whalebone arch. Inside are flags and relics of earlier conflicts. Consecrated in 1892, the cathedral for many years had responsibility for leadership of the Anglican parishes on the mainly Roman Catholic South American mainland.

The Falklands have a rich maritime heritage featured in its greatly expanded Falkland Islands Museum and a separate Dockyard Museum. The Falkland Islands Maritime Heritage Trust (FIMHT) has carried out intensive research, led by a Falkland Islander expert, Mensun Bound, into these wrecks, both merchant and military, on land and deep on the ocean bed. Incredibly, years of planning and several failures have led to its most ambitious and world-acclaimed achievement: locating the wreck of Ernest Shackleton's iconic expedition ship *Endurance* 107 years after she was crushed by ice and abandoned in the Weddell Sea in 1915. Shackleton used the Falkland Islands as his base for several rescue missions to save every member of his crew marooned on Elephant Island. *Endurance* was found and photographed in the deep darkness of the ocean bed on 1 March 2022, exactly 100 years to the day since Shackleton's burial in South Georgia after subsequent expeditions. It is hailed as the most historic find in Antarctic maritime history, achieved by an expedition aptly named *Endurance 22* that used ultra-modern search vessels, remote-controlled robot submersibles, and helicopters. The wreck was 3,000 metres (10,000 feet) below the surface ice, fewer than 5 miles from co-ordinates recorded by her captain, Frank Worsley, on the day she was abandoned. The wreck will be preserved intact and untouched as a histological monument. It is an epic final chapter, recalling the Shackleton family motto 'By endurance, we conquer'.

The Falklands' coasts and waters are littered with nearly 180 hulks of wooden sailing ships battered rounding Cape Horn. They are testament to the Islands' key role as a staging post for shipping, whaling, Antarctic exploration, and even ships braving the perilous journey to join in the California Gold Rush, one of which made it only to Goose Green, its final resting place. A famous ship rescued from this maritime graveyard is Isambard Kingdom Brunel's SS *Great Britain*, which was towed back to Britain in 1970 to be restored at her new berth in Bristol where she was built.

Stanley's modern hospital provides a wide range of services. Patients needing complex treatment can get government-funded flights to Chile or the United Kingdom.

The internet is widely used, and sport is popular with Islanders, especially football and horse racing. Shopping has been transformed with many retail outlets, cafes and modernised pubs. Stanley Services, a versatile company offering goods and services ranging from tourism and car hire to wine imports, is part government-owned.

40

NEW GENERATION IN KEY ROLES

Children of war become leaders in peace. Free full-time education.

Investment in the past has been outmatched by investment for the future, giving education priority. The Falkland Islands have an outstanding record, envied worldwide. Education is fully funded by the government, with small rural schools, travelling teachers and distance learning by telephone, a secondary community school in Stanley and a newer college, and courses in United Kingdom colleges and universities with no fee or accommodation costs.

A younger generation, who were children during the Argentine occupation or born during it and since, have made a major contribution to Island life, occupying vital government and professional posts and acting as outspoken ambassadors at the United Nations and in other countries, voicing their right to decide their own future. They express gratitude to the British armed forces for liberating them, as they explain in a booklet entitled *Our Land, Our Future*.

The children of war have become nation-builders in peace in key roles, including:

Rebecca Edwards: Just after the liberation, a school pupil told me of her ambition to become the first Islander to become a doctor. Rebecca Edwards achieved much more than that. After her degree, she was promoted at an early age to be Medical Director of Health for the whole Islands, running the hospital in Stanley, as well as being the mother of several children.

After her effective control of the 2020 coronavirus pandemic, keeping the Islanders largely free of infection, she was awarded an OBE.

Her parents had already given outstanding service to the Islands. Her father, Roger Edwards, fought in the conflict as a Royal Marine attached to the SAS, and her mother was a nurse. They run a farm and both became members of the Legislature.

Stephen Luxton was a member of the Legislature before his appointment as Director of Oil and Gas Development.

Nick Rendell, born during the Argentine occupation, became Government Environment Officer overseeing conservation, vital for wildlife and tourism. With this experience, he joined his family's sheep farm.

Ros Cheek: Principal Crown Counsel and government legal adviser.

Karen Steen: Junior School Head.

James Wallace, Chief Executive of leading fishing company Fortuna, founded by his father, Stuart Wallace.

Simon Hardcastle, pioneer of fish farming, director of a trout hatchery and fish processing factory. Simon's assistant, **Sam Clegg**, has a degree in sustainable aquaculture. **Daniel Fowler** is another expert in sustainable aquaculture and fisheries.

Michael Poole: Fortuna fisheries manager who also managed the fisheries trade organisation and served as a legislator.

Paul Phillips continued his family's farming tradition, as did **Lee Molkenbuhr**, an expert international sheep shearer. **Nyree Heathman** has run a tourism business. Her parents put their farm, Estancia, at the disposal of paratroopers for the capture of Mount Longdon.

Georgina Strange, an experienced photographer, became manager of the New Island nature reserve, a conservation trust charity, founded with her father, artist and naturalist Ian Strange.

Another conservation reserve on New Island has been created by **Tony and Kim Chater**. Tony is an outstanding wildlife artist and photographer. His son, **Tom Chater**, is a government air service pilot married to **Jane Chater**, a helicopter pilot.

Debbie Summers, only 10 in 1982, has used her expertise in tourism and conservation to promote the Falklands abroad. Influential media Islanders are **Corina Ashbridge**, Manager of Radio Broadcasting, and **Lisa Watson**, editor of the *Penguin News* newspaper and public relations expert.

Lisa gave a fascinating insight into the lives of children during the invasion in a booklet entitled *Waking Up to War*, which she literally wrote as an 11-year-old farmer's daughter whose obsession was a love of horses. She describes the terrifying ordeal in graphic detail interspersed with humour. Her writing flair helped her to gain an honours degree in literature.

Lisa's generation emerged from the trauma of war to become nation builders in key jobs in a democracy prospering in peace.

Six months before the conflict's 40th anniversary, the Falklands government demonstrated its confidence in the future, developing schemes for a new port, new houses, extending the road network and internal air services, and a boost for tourism.

41

THE MODERN ARGENTINA

Democracy endures. Country of contrasts – vast natural resources, widespread poverty, record international debt.

As the Falklands prospered under stable government, Argentina was plunged into what the newspapers called a 'catastrophic' political crisis after government loss of seats in elections to Congress. It caused a rift between President Fernández and his powerful Vice-President, Cristina Fernández de Kirchner, over policies to alleviate poverty. A government reshuffle included a change of Minister for the Malvinas, Antarctic and South Atlantic department, taken over by Guillermo Carmona, regarded as more hard line than his predecessor. This signalled even tougher policies on Falklands sovereignty, as did President Fernández in his latest speech to the United Nations criticising UK rejection of sovereignty negotiations.

Since 1982, Argentina's road to recovery has been an unpredictable roller coaster as dictatorship gave way to democracy, punctuated by political and economic crises. In 2000–01, this resulted in meltdown under President Fernando de la Rúa, with five presidents taking and quitting office within just a few days.

Argentina defaulted on the biggest international debt in history, $132 billion, and has still to repay it. I was in Argentina as shuttered banks were damaged by angry protestors demanding access to their money and investments. I witnessed a modern economy slipping back centuries into mediaeval-type bargaining in which a doctor would trade medical treatment for service to his car or people would swap a bag of potatoes for an item of furniture. It was impossible to sell or buy cars, flats and many other commodities.

Yet Argentina's fledgling democracy survived. It did not succumb, as in the past, to another military coup. Stability was restored despite corruption, cronyism and gangster influence on political parties.

President Cristina Fernández de Kirchner (2007–15) became a powerful leader, winning a second term at the age of 58. But her authoritarian style and policies to control the economy and silence critics alienated influential sections of society, including the unions and the media.

Demonstrators again took to the streets objecting to corruption, crime, soaring inflation, shortages in the shops, and currency restrictions as the Argentine peso plummeted in value.

In her campaign against the Falkland Islands, cynics said she was exploiting a popular cause to deflect attention from domestic difficulties, as Galtieri did in 1982. Her presidency ended amid crisis in 2015. She remained a member of Congress, which shielded her from prosecution for alleged corruption. She returned to government as Vice-President in 2019 in a coalition government led by President Alberto Fernández.

Despite its problems, Argentina has many advantages. It is a beautiful country attractive to tourists, with its rivers, lakes, waterfalls and forests, the majestic Andes mountains and the vast fertile plains of the pampas sustaining millions of cattle and sheep.

Its cosmopolitan capital, Buenos Aires, sometimes described as the 'Paris of South America', has wide boulevards and big squares, luxury hotels, and excellent restaurants and pavement cafes. I have enjoyed some of the best meals of my life at many of these restaurants, especially steaks and pizza.

It is rich in culture and music, the birthplace of the tango, and has a well-educated middle class with access to top universities. It has good medical facilities and transport links, modern manufacturing industries, and nuclear power fuelled by plentiful supplies of natural radium. It has vast natural resources with large reserves of shale oil. Grain, meat and wine exports fetch high prices internationally.

Yet, in a land of plenty, many of its 45 million population suffer poverty. Children go hungry and some die of malnutrition in shanty towns. Isolated aboriginal communities, descendants of indigenous peoples exterminated by the Spanish conquerors in previous centuries, live in mud huts, with no running water, sewage or medical services. The influential Roman Catholic Church campaigns against poverty and neglect, as does its Argentine pope, Francis.

The priority for all its governments has been its Falklands sovereignty claim, on which it has spent vast sums of money, internationally and domestically, bombarding every schoolchild with propaganda. But its campaign eschews military aggression as practised by the dictatorship.

42

ANGLO-ARGENTINE DILEMMAS

Anglo-Argentines torn between loyalty to Argentina and affection for Britain.

The conflict and consequent anti-British sentiment caused anguish in Argentina for what was one of the largest English-speaking communities outside the Commonwealth, whose families had lived there for generations and had allegiances to both sides. Many were educated in English-run schools. One Anglo-Argentine told me: 'We are split personalities. We love Argentina and we love the British.' The conflict created tensions with Argentine friends and threats from demonstrators shouting 'Death to the British'.

Britain had been prominent in nation-building in Argentina, in commerce, banking, insurance, telephones, gas and electricity, tea planting and building railways. Welsh immigrants became involved in sheep farming in Patagonia, where some of their 70,000 descendants still speak Welsh.

Scots developed the beef industry. They imported the first Aberdeen Angus cattle nearly two centuries ago – two heifers called 'Aunt Lee' and 'Cinderella' and a bull aptly named 'Virtuoso'. Millions of Aberdeen Angus now roam the vast pampas grasslands, producing Argentina's favourite steaks. An Argentine whisky brand is called 'Aberdeen Angus'.

The British introduced Argentina's favourite sports: football, rugby, cricket, horse racing and polo. The Hurlingham Club is a sports venue like a little piece of England plonked into Buenos Aires. One of the city's most attractive squares, Plaza Britannica, has a clock tower chiming like Big Ben in London, presented by the British to Argentina. After the conflict, it was renamed 'Air Force Square' in tribute to Argentina's pilots. Many other British names were changed.

English fathers who had fought in the 1939 war for Britain saw their Argentine-born sons go off to fight the British. Some British women married to Argentines had brothers serving with the British forces.

As a consequence of the conflict, Argentina threatened expropriation of British-owned farms and more than 100 British companies which employed thousands of people.

The Anglican Bishop of Buenos Aires, Dr Richard Cutts, wanted to lead a delegation to the occupied islands to tell them what 'a good life the English community enjoyed in Argentina'.

43

SUPPING WITH THE DEVIL

UK negotiated with dictatorship guilty of kidnap, torture and mass murder.

Argentina's 1982 defeat unleashed evidence of the enormity of its human rights crimes against its own population and who committed them. It took many more years before they faced trial. Torture was rife in secret cells close to the British Embassy, and to plush ministerial offices and luxury hotels where British ministers and officials were negotiating to hand over the Falkland Islanders to Argentina, whose Constitution claims to protect everyone's human rights. The British government told the Islanders they would enjoy 'a better life' under Argentine rule – the Islanders knew better!

When I interviewed General Mario Menéndez, he claimed he had treated the Islanders well as Military Governor. Thirty years later, his guilty past in Argentina was exposed in 2012. Aged 82, he was jailed for crimes against humanity. He ran torture and extermination centres holding 1,500 detainees during the so-called 'Operation Independence' in 1975 to crush Marxist revolutionaries.

The strongman of the 1976–83 military juntas was General Jorge Rafael Videla. As President, he launched the systematic killing campaign that condemned an estimated 30,000 Argentines to hideous torture and painful, premature death. He visited the Falklands after the invasion, as did Galtieri.

Videla's coup in 1976 ousted the civilian president, Isabel Perón, and suspended democracy, human rights, free speech, Congress, political parties and trade unions.

I was based in Buenos Aires during Videla's terror campaign. Despite his deceptive appearance of an avuncular Roman Catholic family man devotedly attending Mass, he presided over a maniacal military machine conducting abductions, torture, and mass murder in more than 500 clandestine concentration camps and torture centres. I repeatedly broadcast about their crimes, but their cynical reaction was to dismiss them as 'excesses'.

Their National Reorganisation Process (the 'Proceso') was a euphemism for what we journalists called the 'Dirty War'. Videla said it was 'a war to stamp out subversion at any cost'. He crushed two rebel organisations, the People's Revolutionary Army (Ejército Revolucionario del Pueblo or ERP) and the Peronist Montoneros, who were attacking and killing the military.

But the regime's kidnap squads were given a wider remit to capture 'all subversives, or their sympathisers, associates or anyone who might oppose the government'. This indiscriminately swept into their net a wide swathe of the innocent public, intellectuals, lawyers, students, trade unionists, artists, journalists, nuns and priests, including members of the Jesuit Order then headed by the priest who was to become Pope Paul. There was no public indication that he tried to protect them.

The kidnap squads roamed the streets in unmarked Ford Falcon cars with no number plates. Their victims disappeared, most never to be seen again. They were officially classified as the 'unaccountable missing' or '*desaparecidos*', terrifying new words in the lexicon of state terrorism.

Amnesty International condemned the regime's 'gross violation of human rights'. So, later, did the Argentine National

Commission on the Disappearance of Persons (CONADEP). Its report, entitled '*Nunca Más*' ('Never Again'), quoted, in chilling detail, the testimonies of the survivors.

CONADEP was set up by the post-conflict civilian government, led by lawyer Raúl Alfonsín of the Radical Civic Union, elected in December 1983. But military officers exerted pressure to bring in measures to shield the perpetrators, a law of 'due obedience' excusing junior officers for crimes committed while obeying orders, and a 'full stop law' halting prosecution. In 1990, a general amnesty voided earlier sentences. Much later, the Kirchner governments swept aside these decrees to permit new trials. More than 1,600 officers were tried or accused, another 220 died awaiting trial, and at least fifty went on the run, sought by international arrest warrants.

Nine Argentine leaders of juntas with which the United Kingdom held Falklands sovereignty talks were jailed for mass abduction, torture and executions. Videla was jailed for life, aged 85, and given another fifty-year sentence specifically for the theft of babies stolen from pregnant prisoners forced to give birth while shackled and hooded. They never saw their babies. The mothers' bodies were dumped at sea from military aircraft. An estimated 500 stolen babies were given to military families. Other military officers involved in baby theft were jailed.

Videla showed no remorse. He admitted full responsibility, saying his subordinates were obeying instructions. Videla's junta colleague, Admiral Emilio Massera, was so evil he regarded Videla as 'soft'. His life sentence was cut short by a stroke.

General Galtieri and Admiral Anaya had cancer and died from heart attacks while awaiting trial. Previously, they were sentenced in 1986 to twelve years in prison for mishandling the war. The junta was criticised for picking 'the worst moment' to invade and for 'defective planning'. The Argentine army's internal investigation recommended that Galtieri and Anaya face a firing squad.

Galtieri, born to a poor family of Italian immigrants, graduated from the United States' School of the Americas in Panama, notorious for training many of Latin America's worst dictators. A judge ruled his presidency as 'illegal'. A frail old man, he died in 2003, aged 76. Like many officers guilty of the murder of mothers and teenagers, he was a family man with a wife, a son and two daughters.

Admiral Jorge Isaac Anaya, the son of a medical doctor, was the driving force behind the invasion and bore much of the blame for the defeat. His defensive deployment of his ships left the Royal Navy in control of the seas. He had lived in London during a spell as naval attaché.

A family man with a wife and four daughters, he was implicated in torture, mass murder and the disappearance of thousands of victims as director of the notorious navy mechanics school, ESMA (Escuela Superior de Mecánica de la Armada). From its dungeons, only 100 survived out of an estimated 5,000. After torture, they were classified as '*trasladadas*' – literally 'transferred', a euphemism for 'murdered' – a sinister word reminiscent of the Nazi death camps as many were herded onto the playing field to be cremated on what was called the 'Grill'. ESMA is now a museum, which I visited to see where the awful crimes I had reported were carried out.

Anaya died in 2008, aged 81. The remaining member of the invasion junta, Air Force Brigadier Lami Dozo, died in 2017, aged 88.

A naval pilot, Adolfo Scilingo, confessed in a book called *The Flight* (*El Vuelo*), to participating in 'death flights' from which drugged, naked prisoners were thrown into the Atlantic Ocean. At his trial in Spain, aged 58, his sentences totalled 640 years concurrently for multiple crimes of genocide and terrorism. Interviewed in jail by my daughter, Heather Briley, he said he felt no remorse. About 150 men were tried abroad, in their absence, for murdering about 400 citizens of Spain, Italy, Germany and Sweden.

Sentenced to life imprisonment was Alfredo Astiz, a naval captain who signed the surrender of part of the South Georgia garrison, but first tried, waving a white flag, to lure British officers approaching for surrender talks to walk over mines he had planted. They avoided his trap.

He practised the same evil cunning in Argentina. Using a false identity, he infiltrated human rights organisations to single out victims, including Azucena Villaflor, a founder of the Mothers of the Plaza de Mayo group, and two French nuns, Léonie Duquet and Alice Domon, callously called the 'flying nuns' after their bodies were dumped into the sea from a navy plane. To his victims the blond, baby-faced captain was known as 'the Angel of Death'. He said he was not at all repentant for fighting what he called 'anti-Argentine Marxist terrorists'.

The last military president, General Reynaldo Bignone, who negotiated transition to civilian rule, ordered evidence of the 'Dirty War' to be destroyed. He was jailed for twenty-five years, aged 82.

It was the end of an era of brutal military rule, but not for their victims. Their torment goes on.

44

THE DISAPPEARED WHO WON'T GO AWAY

Mothers and grandmothers plead for lost children, justice and recovery of babies snatched at birth.

The Mothers of the Plaza de Mayo were the most visible symbol of protest against tyranny for four decades. They routinely demonstrate wearing white headscarves, embroidered with the names of their children and the date they disappeared. The headscarves, originally worn to identify each other, became their badge of courage and sorrow. Every week, on Thursday afternoon, since 1976, the Mothers demonstrated in the Plaza de Mayo in front of the Presidential Palace. A sister group, the Grandmothers of the Plaza de Mayo, was formed in 1977 after the devastating discovery of how newborn babies of murdered mothers were stolen and adopted by their tormentors. Those babies, in adulthood, have been discovering to their horror that the 'parents' who brought them up were not their real parents but linked to their biological mothers' murderers.

The Grandmothers' mission has been to trace the stolen children, identify them by genetic DNA tests, and return them to their natural families. The experience has been traumatic, emotional, and deeply disturbing for these children, now adults, torn by mixed feelings and loyalties. More than 120 have been traced and identified, leaving hundreds of others unaware they too may have been stolen at birth.

One high-profile case was a baby who became an elected member of the ruling Congress. Victoria Donda did not discover her real identity until she was 27 years old. She was born in ESMA, where her mother had been tortured and disappeared, along with Victoria's father.

Victoria did not know she had a sister, then a year old, who escaped the kidnappers to be brought up by her grandmother. Victoria sought help from an organisation for the children of the disappeared called HIJOS (*Hijos y Hijas por la Identidad y la Justicia contra el Olvido y Silencio*; Children for Identity and Justice Against Oblivion and Silence). DNA tests confirmed that she was the first lost baby to be identified through her sister.

Victoria was brought up by an officer at the Navy School, Juan Antonio Azic, who in 2011 was jailed for life. Victoria became a human rights campaigner and entered politics. She said: 'My pregnant mother fought for the same decent society I am fighting for, and suffered torture so I could be born.'

The President of the Grandmothers' group, Estela de Carlotto, aged over 90, took even longer to trace her kidnapped grandson, Guido. Her thirty-five-year search ended in 2014 when he was located and identified at the age of 36, a talented pianist and director of a music school.

The Mothers and Grandmothers demanded justice for their children who disappeared without trace and for their grandchildren who disappeared but did not die. Images of their headscarves and their footprints have been painted in white on the stone paving of the square worn smooth by the circular path they walked for so long.

I regularly joined them during the dangerous years of the dictatorship and since, and was photographed from the windows of the State Security headquarters overlooking the square. Interviewing the mothers, I could sense their intense sadness, made more intolerable by the lack of any grave at which to grieve. I also interviewed some of the mothers of the young sailors who died in the *Belgrano*. Their sons lie together as comrades in a hallowed war grave on the ocean bed. Their mothers had only one question: why had they died?

Many of the innocent civilians murdered by the regime also lie on the ocean bed. Their mothers had not one question, but many. Not just why, but how and where and by whom? One mother I interviewed sent her two teenage children to neighbouring Uruguay for safety, but, she tearfully told me, they also disappeared there, where the military regime co-operated with the Argentine junta. This brotherhood of brutality bridged national borders.

Decades later, the names of the victims were painstakingly inscribed on a memorial stone wall on the outskirts of Buenos Aires, half a mile long, overlooking the cold waters of the River Plate where many of them were dumped. The names of some young women are marked '*embarazada*', Spanish for 'pregnant'. I was shown the bare wooden floors of the 'maternity' ward in ESMA where the pregnant mothers were forced to lie down and give birth. Their heads were hooded so that they never even caught a glimpse of their newborn babies. This memorial to Argentina's murdered civilians is located in a lonely, windswept promontory, in contrast to the triumphal city centre memorial to Argentine servicemen killed in the 1982 war, with a perpetual flame of remembrance and a twenty-four-hour guard from the armed forces.

The dictators' victims came from many walks of life, including footballers from famous clubs, which in 2021 supported the families of missing young footballers by granting them honorary membership of their clubs.

SECTION FIVE: EARLY HISTORY, ORIGINS OF DISPUTE

45

DISCOVERY AND SETTLEMENT

Sighted by British navigators. French, Spanish and British settlements. Fact and fiction.

The prolonged sovereignty dispute involved Spain and France in the past as well as Britain and Argentina. It has been complicated by misconceptions, contradictions, and deliberate distortion. Recent detailed research has clarified the facts from documents analysed in archives in Argentina, Britain and the United States.

Britain argues that it claims possession of the Islands by discovery, settlement and peaceful development for two centuries, interrupted only by the 1982 invasion. British families have lived there for ten generations, much longer than many of Argentina's European settlers.

In 1592, the Islands were sighted by passing vessels, including that of a British navigator, John Davis, in his ship *Desire*, whose name is incorporated in the official Falklands emblem 'Desire the Right'. The Islands were unnamed, unmapped and uninhabited.

In 1690, British seamen were the first to set foot on the uninhabited Islands. Their captain, John Strong, named them after Viscount Falkland, Treasurer of the Navy. The Argentine name, Las Malvinas, is a Spanish derivative of a French name, Les Îles Malouines, used by seaman from their home fishing port of Saint-Malo.

In 1764, the first small settlement was established by French explorer, Louis Antoine de Bougainville, followed soon afterwards by British and Spanish settlements.

In 1765, Commodore John Byron claimed possession for the British Crown. This prompted a protest from Spain, which had conquered and colonised much of South America and massacred the indigenous Amerindian populations.

Spain, which appointed a governor based in Buenos Aires, forced the French to leave, and then the British in 1770. But in 1771, the British settlement was re-established in Port Egmont in West Falkland. The Spanish withdrew from their Port Louis settlement in East Falkland in 1811 without any legal handover to the Buenos Aires authorities.

Spain's claim dated back much earlier to an autocratic declaration in 1492 by a Spanish pope, Alexander, that all territories discovered in the New World (meaning the Americas) and much of the Pacific belonged to Spain. In response to a protest from Portugal, it was apportioned a share by Pope Alexander. He was no normal pope but notorious for his corruption, greed and promiscuity.

He had no legitimate, moral or divine right to issue such anachronistic decrees. No one now, not even the Vatican, regards his declaration as valid, issued a century before the Falkland Islands were known to exist.

In 1816, five years after Spain withdrew its Falklands settlement, Argentina declared independence from Spain as the United Provinces of the River Plate, claiming inheritance of former Spanish territory.

Official archives reveal that when Britain granted recognition in 1825 to the new nation that became Argentina, it was on the basis of its own Foreign Ministry's definition of its territory, which did *not* include the Falkland Islands.

It was not until 1826 (sixty-one years after Britain claimed possession) that the first Argentine foray established a presence in the Falklands. This was a private venture by a Buenos Aires citizen, Louis Vernet, to hunt cattle for meat and hides. Argentina appointed Vernet as its unpaid 'civil and military commandant' and encouraged him to set up a colony and claim fishery rights.

The United States clashed with Vernet after he seized three American sealing ships. The American sloop *Lexington* destroyed his settlement and escorted his employees back to Buenos Aires. The Americans denounced Vernet as a pirate, disputed the claim that Spain had transferred its possessions to Buenos Aires, and declared the Falkland Islands to be 'free of all government'.

In 1832, the Governor of Buenos Aires dispatched a garrison of twenty-six soldiers with their families to reinforce Argentina's claim. But the Argentine garrison commander, Captain Jean Etienne Mestivier, was murdered by mutineers. Britain sent a naval ship, HMS *Clio*, to restore order. Her captain, John James Onslow, replaced the Buenos Aires flag with the Union Jack. He sent back to Argentina the mutineers and the military garrison, some of whom were executed.

This is the action which Argentina alleges usurped its sovereignty by evicting the 'resident' Argentine population. This is untrue, as proved by archives in Argentina, Britain and the United States. Captain Onslow had orders *not* to expel the civilian population and invited them to remain, most of them Argentines. The 150th anniversary of this incident was Argentina's deadline for the acquisition of sovereignty and led to the 1982 invasion.

In 1833, gauchos led by Antonio Rivero murdered British officials in charge of the Islands, William Dickson and Matthew Brisbane, and three others, including an Argentine. British ships again arrived to restore order. Lieutenant Henry Smith was left in charge. Rivero and his gaucho gang were evicted. Rivero is hailed as a hero by Argentina.

A treaty called the Convention of Peace ratified by Argentina and Britain in 1850 was accepted as resolving all disputes between them, including the Falklands, which was hardly mentioned for nearly a century.

Argentina has implanted its sovereignty claim ever deeper into its Constitution, its laws, and the minds of its citizens. Monuments, a new multimillion-dollar Malvinas Museum, and school books inculcate the theme that '*Las Malvinas son nuestras*' ('the Malvinas are ours').

46

BYGONE BATTLES

**Naval battles. Secret wartime 'Operation Tabarin'.
Vital Antarctic base. Formation of British Antarctic Survey.**

Geography, as well as history, shaped the Falkland Islands' destiny. In the era of sailing ships, they were for centuries a welcome haven for vessels braving violent seas as they rounded Cape Horn. This shipping route declined when the Panama Canal opened in 1914, providing easier passage between the Atlantic and Pacific oceans.

The Islands were ideally located for Antarctic exploration and research and for naval operations. The Royal Navy had a central role in discovering, settling and defending the Islands, not least in clashes with Germany in both world wars.

The Royal Navy suffered its most disastrous defeat for over 100 years in the Battle of Coronel in the Pacific off Chile, on 1 November 1914. Admiral Graf von Spee's East Asian Squadron sank two cruisers, *Good Hope* and *Monmouth*, with all hands lost, more than 1,600 dead including their commander, Rear-Admiral Sir Christopher Cradock. The Falkland Islands' gold reserves of £3,750, lent by the Governor to Cradock, went down with his ship.

This defeat was avenged five weeks later in one of the Royal Navy's most decisive victories ever in the Battle of the Falkland Islands, on 8 December 1914. All five of Graf von Spee's battle cruisers and his three support ships were vanquished, and all but one of them sunk with nearly 2,000 men killed, including Admiral Graf von Spee and his two sons. No British ships were lost, and only eleven British sailors were killed.

Graf von Spee's squadron had been a threat to commercial shipping and to troopships sailing to Europe from Australia and New Zealand.

The Admiralty deployed a powerful force to the South Atlantic – eight cruisers and a battleship, *Canopus*, under the command of Rear Admiral Sir Doveton Sturdee. The German squadron rounded Cape Horn intending to destroy the Falkland's base installations.

Admiral von Spee, believing the Falklands were undefended, was confronted by the powerful British force that had arrived only the previous day. Von Spee beat a rapid retreat to no avail. A memorial statue in Stanley commemorates Admiral Sturdee's victory, and a new memorial wall commemorating both battles was erected in Stanley for the 100th anniversary in 2014.

Memories of the battle were rekindled in 2019 when the wreck of the Admiral's flagship *Scharnhorst* was located on the ocean bed by divers from the Falklands Maritime Trust, led by deep sea expert Mensun Bound.

The 1914 battles had an echo in the first major naval battle of the Second World War; again in the South Atlantic, in December 1939. The powerful German battleship *Admiral Graf Spee*, named after the First World War commander, which had sunk several British merchant ships, was hunted down, engaged and defeated in the Battle of the River Plate by a Falklands-based force commanded by Commodore Henry Harwood. His two smaller cruisers, HMS *Exeter* and *Ajax*, along with HMS *Achilles*, a New Zealand warship, fought the more powerful Graf Spee to a standstill, forcing her into Montevideo in Uruguay. Her captain, Hans Langsdorff, scuttled his ship to avoid loss of more lives. Langsdorff committed suicide in Buenos Aires.

I was the only journalist invited to the 40th anniversary reconciliation reunion of River Plate veterans from both sides in Montevideo. Winston Churchill, as First Lord of the Admiralty at the beginning of both world wars, oversaw all three battles.

In 1944, a clandestine wartime mission, codenamed Operation Tabarin, was tasked to establish permanent British bases in the Antarctic and deter enemy activity.

Operation Tabarin led to the formation of the British Antarctic Survey (BAS), an organisation of unrivalled scientific and environmental expertise, with hundreds of staff and several bases and research ships in Antarctica, the latest named *Sir David Attenborough*, deployed from 2022.

A remarkable international accord, the Antarctic Treaty, has preserved peace and the environment and prevented economic exploitation for decades.

APPENDIX 1

INTERVIEW WITH ARGENTINE FOREIGN MINISTER DR NICANOR COSTA MÉNDEZ

Falklands war 'a mistake'

In an exclusive post-conflict Buenos Aires interview never previously published, the Argentine Foreign Minister, Doctor Costa Mendez, said Argentina's invasion of the Falklands Islands was meant only to force negotiations. General Galtieri never wanted to fight a war and intended twice to withdraw the invasion force. Here are the Foreign Minister's own words as a unique retrospective contribution to the debate:

Harold Briley: When did you first learn that the military chiefs wanted to take the Falklands?

Dr Costa Mendez: On February 13th, 1982, President Galtieri in one of our routine weekly meetings said not that they had made any decision on invading or occupying the Islands but that they were making military preparations just in case the government may need to occupy the Islands, as a contingency preparation. I asked whether that meant I should make some diplomatic preparations or I had to study the case to see whether it was possible from the legal or diplomatic point of view. He said, 'No.'

HB: When did you know an invasion was to take place?

CM: I won't ever forget. It was exactly on the 26th March. I was given strict orders not to communicate this news to anyone on the civilian side, in order to keep the secret for two main reasons, because of security and because of success. I said it can be if it is done just to occupy the Islands and immediately begin negotiations under the United Nations or the Organisation of American States or any other mediator. We thought that occupying the Islands would press Britain to negotiate or press the international organisations to intervene and try to obtain a peaceful end of a quarrel and a conflict. We wanted to speed up negotiations. We thought Britain was procrastinating. The plan did not work because of its success. When the government occupied the Islands, the enthusiasm in Argentina was tremendous. The occupation was a great success. The government was a prisoner of its success and was not free enough to negotiate and follow its original plan which was to withdraw the troops and call for United Nations troops to occupy during the negotiations. That was the original plan.

The problem of the success of the occupation – peaceful with no blood being spilt – changed the plans. We had no desire of fighting a war against Britain. The negotiation had been stalled for so many years, something should be done to speed up and show Britain it should pay attention to this problem, otherwise it would run out of control.

HB: So the war was a mistake really?

CM: The war was a mistake. I do not want to pass judgment on foreign governments. But Mrs Thatcher precipitated things when she took too early the decision to send the fleet. That decision, given the tensions and general spirit in Argentina, provoked a harder, tougher attitude in Argentina.

HB: What else could she have done at that stage?

CM: She could have delayed that decision for some days and tried to see if Argentina's original idea could have been worked out and so let the United Nations troops take over.

HB: She did not know that. She thought the Argentines had taken the Islands with the intention of keeping them.

CM: This is not what we publicly said in the junta's declaration. It was a surprise that the British government took a definite decision and reacted with the last possibility, the ultimate option, the last resort. I am sure Britain would not have lost anything by waiting. War is tremendously complicated and every government loses control over a war from its beginning. There are so many things involved in a war. One was the internal situation of the British government. Argentina's government was trying to obtain some support from public opinion. And Mrs Thatcher was at the lowest point of her popularity. I think she reacted so toughly because she thought, and thought right, that reacting that way would rally around her public opinion.

Argentina wanted UN Resolution

CM: The United Nations' resolution was, in a way, what we wanted, a very compelling invitation to negotiate. We presented a written note agreeing to a resolution.

HB: If you had withdrawn your troops, would it not have achieved what you wanted in the first place?

CM: Yes, but we wanted some assurances before withdrawing the troops, assurances that the discussions would be quick, that a resolution would be obtained by the end of the year. I was asked on a United States TV programme, *Face the Nation,* is recognition of Argentina's sovereignty a condition of negotiations? I very clearly said, 'No.' Argentina is ready to begin negotiations without prejudices and without prejudgment. We wanted to negotiate sovereignty. We did not say we wanted to negotiate recognition. We did not say it was a precondition that Argentina must have sovereignty.

HB: What was your view of the United States' attempt to mediate, particularly Secretary of State Al Haig.

CM: It was a move we thought, before the occupation, an expected move by the American government. I think we were unlucky in the choice of [General Al Haig as] the mediator. Perhaps [Vice President George] Bush or Mrs Kirkpatrick [US ambassador to the United Nations] could have been better negotiators.

HB: Mrs Kirkpatrick was very pro-Argentine.

CM: Mrs Kirkpatrick and most of the staff of the State Department were in favour of trying to reach an agreement and not giving full support to Britain.

Mr Reagan made a great mistake in thinking that as Mr Haig was a general; he could talk to the Argentine generals in a very special professional language and by that way reach agreement. Mr Haig proved to be a very awkward mediator. He tried to resemble his great master, Mr Kissinger, but he resembled him only in his flights around the world … shuttle diplomacy.

HB: I thought you meant flights of imagination.

CM: No, he had no imagination whatsoever. He was not what we expected – an honest broker.

A different mediator could have avoided the war. It was not easy. He was acting in good faith. The problem is he did not understand the problem. He did not know how to manage the problem.

HB: He did not have the right qualities and attitude? He found, after all, that as a general, he was not able to communicate or understand the Argentine military?

CM: There was no rapport. He was a very tough critic of the Argentine generals. I should have fought more for peace and negotiations and pressed the government to avoid or postpone the invasion and to try every means to end the conflict in a peaceful way. With hindsight I did not do enough. I did not fight for a peaceful solution to the conflict more.

HB: Once that quick victory had been obtained, the invasion so easily without bloodshed, you were then a prisoner?

CM: In a way yes. President Galtieri saw very clearly that. On two occasions, General Galtieri called me and said I think we should withdraw from the Islands, the first time by the end of April. He called me in New York and the second time was around May 15th.

HB: Why did that not happen?

CM: In the first place, precisely because the bombardment of the Islands on the first of May prevented his decision being carried out.

HB: If that had not happened, you might have withdrawn?

CM: He called me and told me to prepare everything in order to announce to the Security Council that Argentina would accept the Council's decision and withdraw from the Islands.

HB: That is amazing. That has not been revealed before, has it? And the second time — why did it not happen?

CM: The second time there was more opposition within the military in Argentina.

HB: By that time, there had been a fair bit of fighting. What about the initiative by President Belaunde Terry of Peru?

CM: That was an excellent initiative. We were on the verge of accepting it when the sinking of the *Belgrano* occurred. I am sure that any of the three great initiatives could have succeeded – Haig, Belaunde Terry and Perez de Cuellar [UN Secretary General].

But the big stumbling block on the road to peace was the problem of self-determination of the Islanders, because Britain said there was no way of resolving the problem without respecting fully the self-determination problem, the wishes of the Islanders to stay British. If Argentina said yes, if we accept that proposition, we would accept that legally the British are entitled to have the islands. There was no way – it was catch-22.

HB: You have democracy now in Argentina. Was there not some strength in that argument, that there should be self-determination? Don't you think that the Islanders should have had some wish or say in this?

CM: They should have every possibility of publicly expressing their points of view. We were ready and we are still ready – and every [Argentine] government has ratified this, that we are ready for the Islands to be governed under British rules, that the rules on laws, on marriage, on divorce, on education and the language should be maintained, and to give the largest possible participation to the Islanders in the Islands' institutions, organisations and so forth. I think the greatest idea on the Malvinas problem was given by Lord Chalfont in 1968. A charming man, very intelligent, very shrewd, who knew the problem. He proposed to us the lease-back solution.

HB: Which Nicholas Ridley proposed later on.

CM: He failed in one of the greatest failures in the history of the Malvinas.

HB: Why did he fail?

CM: There were many backbenchers in the Conservative Party who were against. And very intelligently, very ably, moved by the Falklands lobby, an excellent lobby. The greatest problem now is economic and should be solved in economic terms. I do not fully understand why Britain is so interested in keeping those Islands so far from home, so uninteresting from the point of view of world politics, with no strategic meaning today, with no military significance. It is still a mystery why Britain has fought so furiously for those islands.

HB: They are home to the Islanders. They have been afraid of the military in Argentina, as some Argentines have been.

CM: I believe that if Lord Carrington and myself could have spoken just a few words before the invasion, the invasion could at least have been postponed. [Harold Briley later put this view to Lord Carrington, who disagreed.] I think that some joint ventures could have been created that could have perhaps created a better climate to negotiate. The opening of the communications did not work [an initiative by Ted Heath's 1970 government]. Seduction: yes. Rape: no. We still want sovereignty.

HB: Argentina has secured democracy. Now that you are democratic, don't you see a case for the Islanders to be democratic?

CM: A full case. To respect Argentina's sovereignty, having all their rights to live in peace.

HB: But not the Falkland Islanders to have their wishes and rights and self-determination?

CM: We are the owners of the land.

HB: There is dispute over ownership of the land.

APPENDIX 2

HISTORY DATE MILESTONES

1492	Spanish Pope Alexander declares most of the 'New World' in the Americas and much of the Pacific belongs to Spain and Portugal.
1494	Spain and Portugal agree to share the Americas, defining their territories each side of what was called the Tordesillas Line. This bilateral agreement and the Pope's declaration were rejected by other European countries.
1592	First recorded sighting of the Falkland Islands by the English navigator John Davis in his ship *Desire*, whose name is incorporated in the Islands' flag and motto 'Desire the Right', denoting democracy and fairness.
1690	First recorded landing, by British captain John Strong aboard *Welfare*. He named the channel between the main islands 'Falkland Sound' after Viscount Falkland, Treasurer of the Navy.
1764	French explorer Louis Antoine de Bougainville establishes a settlement at Port Louis on East Falkland.

1765	Commodore John Byron lands at Port Egmont on West Falkland and claims possession for the British Crown. Captain John MacBride establishes settlement there in 1766.
1766	Spanish government protests about French settlement, which Bougainville is forced to surrender to rule by a Spanish governor under jurisdiction of Captain-General of Buenos Aires, then a Spanish colony.
1770	Britain forced from Port Egmont by Spain.
1771	Port Egmont restored to Britain by agreement with Spain and France.
1774	Britain withdraws for economic reasons leaving behind a plaque claiming continuing British sovereignty.
1806/ 1807	Two failed British invasions of the River Plate in Argentina.
1811	Spanish garrison withdraws from Port Louis which they had renamed Puerto de la Soledad.
1816	Argentina declares independence from Spain as United Provinces of the River Plate.
1825	Britain officially recognises the Buenos Aires government whose Foreign Ministry defined its geographical boundaries, which excluded the Falkland Islands. A friendship and trade agreement signed by both governments, with no mention of the Falklands.

1826	Naturalised Buenos Aires citizen Louis Vernet privately establishes a settlement in the Falklands at Puerto de la Soledad.
1829	Buenos Aires appoints Vernet unpaid 'Commander' and claims all rights in the region previously exercised by Spain. Britain formally protests, asserting its sovereignty over the Falklands.
1831	Vernet seizes three American sealing ships in attempt to control fishing. US sloop *Lexington* destroys his settlement and proclaims the Islands 'free of all government'.
1832	US questions the claim that all Spanish possessions had been transferred to the government of Buenos Aires. Buenos Aires appoints an interim governor in the Falklands, Commander Mestivier, who is murdered by his own mutinous soldiers.
January 1833	Captain Onslow in HMS *Clio* reclaims possession of Islands for Britain and expels mutinous garrison. Buenos Aires protests that an Argentine resident population is expelled. This is untrue, as all Argentine citizens, including gauchos, were permitted to remain.
August 1833	Argentine gauchos led by Antonio Rivero murder British officials in charge of Islands, William Dickson and Matthew Brisbane, and three others including an Argentine.

January 1834	British ships visit and Lieutenant Henry Smith left in charge as first British Governor. Rivero and gaucho gang arrested and expelled to Uruguay.
1845	Port Louis replaced as capital by Stanley, named after Edward Stanley, Earl of Derby.
1850	Britain and Buenos Aires governments ratify Convention of Settlement of all existing disagreements and re-establishment of friendship, with no mention of the Falkland Islands.
1853	Republic of Argentina established.
1914	Panama Canal opens so ships can cross between the Pacific and the Atlantic without rounding Cape Horn, so reducing the value of the Falkland Islands for shipping.
November 1914	Battle of Coronel, off the Chilean coast, two British warships fleet commanded by Admiral Cradock sunk by German fleet led by Admiral Graf von Spee.
December 1914	Battle of the Falklands. Admiral von Spee's fleet sunk by Royal Navy fleet led by Admiral Sturdee.
December 1939	Battle of the River Plate. Falklands flotilla of *Exeter*, *Ajax* and *Achilles* force German battleship *Graf Spee* to scuttle off Montevideo. *Cumberland* replaces *Exeter*, badly damaged, returns to Falklands.

1942	Garrison of 2,000 (West Yorkshire Regiment) sent to defend Islands to deter threat of Japanese invasion.
1944	First British bases in Antarctic in wartime expedition 'Operation Tabarin' to deter access to anchorages by enemy ships and strengthen Britain's claim to the Falkland Islands dependencies. Its scientific research developed into a world-class organisation, the British Antarctic Survey (BAS).
1944	BBC radio programme *Calling the Falklands* went on air for next sixty-two years, axed in 2006.
December 1965	UN General Assembly resolution (2065) calls on UK and Argentina to negotiate peaceful solution to sovereignty dispute. Debated annually by UN Committee of 24 (Decolonisation Committee).
1966	Anglo-Argentine talks start between Harold Wilson's Labour government and Argentina.
1967	Falkland Islands Emergency Committee (later Falkland Islands Association) founded in London to campaign against surrender of sovereignty.
1971	Communications agreement by UK (Prime Minister Edward Heath) for Argentina to provide oil supplies and an air link from Southern Argentina.

1976	Lord Shackleton's first Falklands economic survey. His ship fired upon by Argentine warship.
April 1982	Argentine invasion.
May 1982	British task force land at San Carlos.
14 June 1982	Argentine surrender. Islands liberated. Lord Shackleton updates Economic Review.
January 1983	Official (Lord Franks) inquiry clears Thatcher government of blame for invasion.
1983	Argentine military surrender power to civilian government headed by Raúl Alfonsín (Radical Civic Union).
July 1985	UK Parliament Foreign Affairs Committee Inquiry challenges Franks Report findings, criticises Thatcher government.
1986	UK fails to get regional fishing agreement through the UN Food and Agriculture Organisation.
October 1986	UK declares 200-mile conservation zone enabling commercial fishing to develop as mainstay of Falklands economy.
1990	Diplomatic relations restored between UK and Argentina.
1994	Argentina incorporates sovereignty claim in Constitution for full control over Falkland Islands, South Georgia and South Shetland Islands. This precludes impartial negotiation or compromise.

1995	UK–Argentine agreement on oil exploration in Falklands waters, which encourages oil companies to drill.
1999	UK–Argentina accord, supported by Falklands Legislature, 'to build confidence and reduce tension', negotiated by Foreign Ministers Robin Cook and Guido di Tella for Tony Blair and President Menem governments. Provides for co-operation on fishing and conservation of stocks.
2000	Exploratory oil drilling begins.
2000–01	Argentine economic crisis closes banks, defaults on record foreign debt, with five presidents within a few days.
2007	Cristina Fernández de Kirchner succeeded her husband, Nestor Kirchner, as President. Argentina repudiates 1999 co-operation accord and 1995 oil agreement.
2010	Oil rig resumes drilling in Falklands waters. Argentina imposes shipping restrictions, requiring Argentine permits, in attempt to disrupt equipment delivery.
2011	President Cristina Fernández re-elected for second term with record majority.
2011	Argentina intensifies restrictions on fishing boats with Falklands flags, boarding and harassing them, targeting Spanish vessels and threatening fines. Uruguay, Brazil and Chile join in ban and include British warships. Actions condemned by UK as 'internationally unlawful'.

2011–12	Argentina imports oil as domestic supplies diminish.
2012	UK rejects Argentine accusation of 'militarising' South Atlantic. UK insists on adequate defences against threats.
2012	Argentina protests at 'provocation' of Prince William serving as Falklands helicopter search and rescue pilot. UK and international companies dismiss Argentine threats of legal action against oil and other companies involved in Falklands drilling or support services.
March 2013	Landmark Falklands referendum. Landslide 99.8 per cent majority vote to stay British. Argentina refuses to recognise referendum.
2014	Offshore oil discoveries by smaller British companies attract huge investment from international conglomerates. Oil production delay for several years.
2014	Record Falklands squid catch worth £45 million.
December 2015	Argentina elects new president, Mauricio Macri, former Mayor of Buenos Aires, defeating ruling Peronists.
2016	Macri and UK agree more positive relationship. Co-operation agreement on economic, trade, fishery conservation and other issues.

2019	New government of President Alberto Fernández and Vice-President Cristina Fernández reject Macri Agreement, intensify sovereignty claim and introduce punitive laws against Falkland Islands.
2017	United States CIA declassified documents reveal 1982 plan to give Falkland Islands to Argentina to avoid another war.
2021	United States report criticises Argentina's continuing human rights failures, crime and ineffective judiciary.

ACKNOWLEDGEMENTS AND BIBLIOGRAPHY

The author conducted many interviews with leading political and military figures including:

British: Prime Ministers Margaret Thatcher, Edward Heath and James Callaghan; Foreign Office Ministers Lord Carrington and Nicholas Ridley; Defence Secretary John Nott; Falklands Governor Rex Hunt and several other Governors, many Falklands Legislators; government officials, businessmen and residents both before and after the 1982 conflict.

Military Commanders: Admirals Lewin and Woodward; Commander Rick Jolly; Brigadier Julian Thompson; Submarine Commander Wreford-Brown; Air Chief Marshal Peter Squire; Welsh Guardsman Simon Weston, and many other combatants; Mrs Sara Jones, widow of Colonel H. Jones, and other relatives; *Buenos Aires Herald* editors Robert Cox, James Neilson and other journalists.

Argentines: Foreign Ministers Guido de Tella, Generals Menéndez and Jofre; Admirals Carlos Büsser and Lombardo; *Belgrano* Captain Bonzo and other Argentine combatants and widows.

Every effort has been made to confirm copyright holders, and in the event of any omission please contact the author care of the publishers so they may be rectified in future editions.

Official Reports

Franks Islands Review (Franks Committee of Privy Councillors), Command Paper 8787, presented to Parliament, January 1983

House of Commons Foreign Affairs Committee: Two Inquiries with reports – one on the Conflict and its origins, and the second on the sinking of the cruiser Belgrano. (London: HM Stationery Office, 1983–85)

Professor Sir Lawrence Freedman, *The Official History of the Falklands Campaign*, vols 1–2. (Abingdon: Routledge, 2005)

Amnesty International, Argentina, Report of Trial of Junta Members, 1987

Argentine National Commission on the Disappearance of Persons (CONADEP) with its report entitled 'Nunca Más' ('Never Again')

Books

Graham Bound, *Falkland Islanders at War* (Barnsley: Pen and Sword, 1992)

Commodore Michael Clapp and Ewen Southby-Tailyour, *Amphibious Assault Falklands* (Barnsley: Pen and Sword, 1996)

Max Hastings and Simon Jenkins, The *Battle for the Falklands* (London: Pan Books, 1983)

Sir Rex Hunt, *My Falkland Days* (London: David and Charles, 1992)

Bernard Ingham, *Kill the Messenger* (London: Fontana Press, 1991)

Surgeon Commander Rick Jolly, *The Red and Green Life Machine* (London: Century Publishing, 1983)

Jean Seaton, *Pinkoes and Traitors* (London: Profile Books, 2015)

Lisa Watson, *Waking Up to War* (Stanley: Stanley Services Ltd, 2010)

John Wilsey, *H. Jones VC: The Life and Death of an Unusual Hero* (London: Cornerstone 2003)

Margaret Thatcher, The Downing Street Years (London: Harper Collins, 1993)

Brigadier Julian Thompson, *No Picnic* (Barnsley: Pen and Sword, 1985)

John Smith, *74 Days: An Islander's Diary of the Falklands Occupation* (London: Century Publishing, 1984)

Nigel Ward, *Sea Harrier over the Falklands* (Barnsley: Pen and Sword, 1992)

Admiral Sandy Woodward with Patrick Robinson, *One Hundred Days: The Memoirs of the Falklands Battle Group Commander* (London: Harper Collins, 1992)

Media

BBC External Services and the Falklands Crisis, July 1982

BBC Despatches by Brian Hanrahan and Robert Fox with task force, and Harold Briley, Buenos Aires and Falklands 1981–83

Buenos Aires Herald

Falkland Islands Broadcasting Service: Invasion Day radio commentary by Patrick Watts, 1982

MercoPress News Agency and *Penguin News* newspaper

Ministry of Defence

National Archives

I had invaluable help from colleagues in Reuters news agency with their accurate reports, which were totally reliable wherever

I worked in the world. I also had support from Australian freelance reporter John Arden, with whom I worked previously in the Iran and Nicaragua Revolutions. He saved my life more than once.

I would also like to acknowledge the help of the Falkland Islands Government and its London Office (FIGO), Phyllis Rendell (Anniversary Coordinator) and the Falkland Island Association newslettter.

Finally, thanks to my daughter, Heather Briley, who provided invaluable research and internet expertise.

ABOUT THE AUTHOR

Harold Briley was a BBC political, defence and foreign correspondent for thirty years, where he covered the East–West Cold
War and conflicts in Asia, Africa, the Middle East and Central
America, including the 1971 Indo–Pakistan–Bangladesh war, and
the 1979 Iran and Nicaragua Revolutions.

He was the BBC Latin America correspondent from 1979 to
1983, and was based in Argentina throughout the Falklands War.
This gave him a unique insight into the conflict that people still
ask him for today.

Awarded an OBE for services to journalism and broadcasting, after retiring Briley spent twenty years as a member of the
Falkland Islands Association, editing their news magazine and
publications, as well as being involved in press and charity work
all over the globe. He is married with two children and lives in
East Sussex.